STUDY SMART!

Ready-to-Use Reading/Study Skills Activities for Grades 5–12

ANTOINETTE BRESCHER
GARY W. ABBAMONT

illustrated by: Eileen Gerne Ciavarella

THE CENTER FOR APPLIED
RESEARCH IN EDUCATION
West Nyack, New York 10995

Library of Congress Cataloging-in-Publication Data

Abbamont, Gary W., 1951–.
    Study smart! : ready-to-use reading/study skills activities for
grades 5–12 / Gary W. Abbamont and Antoinette Brescher ; illustrated
by Eileen Gerne Ciavarella.
      p. cm.
    ISBN 0-87628-872-7
    1. Reading—Aids and devices. 2. Study, Method of. 3. Teaching—
Aids and devices. I. Brescher, Antoinette, 1947– . II. Center
for Applied Research in Education. III. Title.
LB1573.89.A23   1990   90-33729
371.3'078—dc20   CIP

Printed in the United States of America

15 14 13 12

ISBN 0-87628-872-7

**THE CENTER FOR APPLIED RESEARCH
IN EDUCATION**
West Nyack, NY 10994

On the World Wide Web at http://www.phdirect.com

ABOUT THE AUTHORS

GARY W. ABBAMONT received his B.A. degree from Rutgers University (New Brunswick, NJ) and his M.A. degree in the administration of education programs from Columbia University's Teacher's College (New York, NY).

Since 1973, he has been a teacher of both social studies and language arts at Crossroads Middle School in South Brunswick Township, N.J. He has also been chairperson of the language arts department since 1984.

Mr. Abbamont is a member of the National Council of the Teachers of English and the International Reading Association. In 1987 he was named "Outstanding Educator" in New Jersey's Teacher Recognition Program.

ANTOINETTE BRESCHER holds a B.A. degree in elementary education and a M.A. degree in reading from Kean College (Union, N.J.)

Ms. Brescher has taught grades 4-6 in Montgomery County, MD, and science for grades 7-8 at Crossroads Middle School. She currently teaches science in grades 3-6 at the Gill/St. Bernards School in Bernardsville, N.J.

In addition to her teaching experiences, Ms. Brescher was the reading consultant and a freelancer writer for the Silver Burdett & Ginn Elementary Science series.

THE AUTHORS team-taught together while at Crossroads Middle School. They worked as a team in developing many instructional materials that became the basis for this book. These activities were developed, refined, and tested with several hundred students.

ABOUT THIS TEACHING RESOURCE

"Why didn't I do well on that test? I studied."
"What was number 9 again?"
"Where do I start?"
"Where can I find that information?"

If you work with students in the middle grades, you have undoubtedly heard questions like these many times. Both teachers and students are often frustrated by the poor results caused by students' ineffective study habits and inability to accomplish assigned learning tasks. Both are often frustrated, too, by textbooks and other materials that require students to perform a task without first showing them how.

The purpose of *STUDY SMART! Ready-to-Use Reading/Study Skills Activities for Grades 5-12* is to help you teach your students the reading and study skills they are called on to apply in school every day—skills that are essential to efficient and effective learning of all subjects. Students are many times surprised to find out that strategies exist which can direct them in effective learning. Practice in using these strategies will help them master the skills and apply them to new situations on their own.

For easy use, this resource is organized into four major units: I. DEVELOPING READING SKILLS, II. DEVELOPING STUDY SKILLS, III. LOCATING INFORMATION SKILLS, and IV. CONSTRUCTING GRAPHIC AIDS. Each unit begins with a general overview and is divided into two or more sections focusing on specific skills. Each basic skills section, in turn, begins with notes to the teacher, including the skills, objectives, strategies, teaching hints and answer keys. These are followed by a number of reproducible worksheet activities you can photocopy as many times as needed for individual or group use.

Unit I, DEVELOPING READING SKILLS, provides 64 student worksheet activities to teach and reinforce specific subskills in each of these areas: Recognizing Organization, Adjusting Reading Rate, Reading Graphic Aids, and Developing Vocabulary. The specific subskills covered under Recognizing Organization, for example, include main idea, supporting details, sequence, cause/effect, fact/opinion, conclusions, comparison/contrast, and analogies. Several sample activities are "Writing a Headline," "Creating a Timeline," "Cause-Effects-Solutions," and "Is It an Alligator or a Crocodile?"

Unit II, DEVELOPING STUDY SKILLS, presents 23 worksheet activities to build skills in five areas: Following Directions, Listening, Taking Notes, Studying and Taking Tests, and Doing Homework. Sample activities for Taking Notes include "Listening for Information," "Listening for the Main Parts," "Outlining," "Highlighting," "Key Words," and "Picture It."

Unit III, LOCATING INFORMATION SKILLS, provides 47 student worksheets to teach and reinforce skills in these areas: Using a Textbook, Using the Library, and Reading to Survive. Topics covered under Reading to Survive, for example, include forms, telephone books, newspapers, signs, maps, labels, catalogs, and schedules. Sample newspaper reading activities are "What's in a Weather Map?," "What's the Temperature?," "What's the Main Idea?," "What's the Best Price?," and "Can I Do the Job?"

Unit IV, CONSTRUCTING GRAPHIC AIDS, offers 16 worksheets featuring (A) Pictures, Diagrams and Posters, (B) Tables and Graphs, and (C) Maps and Models. The activities for Tables and Graphs include "Presenting Information Through a Table," "Drawing a Bar Graph," "Drawing a Line Graph," and "Drawing a Circle Graph."

Each reproducible activity is keyed to the section and states the skill covered, the objective, and the procedure to follow in carrying out the activity. In some cases, it also includes a follow-up extension activity. This simple format provides a model for you to develop similar activities. You will find that many of the worksheets can be used more than once. For example, the strategy for finding the main idea of a news article can be used with a limitless number of articles. Repeated use reinforces the skill.

STUDY SMART! Ready-to-Use Reading/Study Skills Activities for Grades 5-12 provides teachers with a ready store of activities to teach and reinforce basic reading and study skills. Its overall aim is to help students understand and develop specific ways to learn. Teaching young people how to learn gives them the awareness and tools they need to take advantage of a lifetime of learning opportunity.

Gary W. Abbamont
Antoinette Brescher

Dedicated to JACK and JOHN,
the joys of my life!

–Toni

Dedicated to
HEIDI ANGELA & JOSEPH P. ABBAMONT,
a loving mom and dad who devoted
their lives to their children
–my finest teachers, my best friends–
and to
JOE and JODI
HEIDI and SCOTT
Timothy James and Christopher Ryan
RICHARD and MARIA
Abby Linn
–a family whose love has been my inspiration–
–Gary

CONTENTS

2. Context Clues

3. Multiple Meanings

Unit II   DEVELOPING STUDY SKILLS

Activity Sheets:

Activity Sheets:

Unit IV CONSTRUCTING GRAPHIC AIDS   **215**

unit *I*

DEVELOPING READING SKILLS

Unit I presents activities to help develop reading skills necessary for learning in the content areas. Students with strong reading skills are better able to read and understand and to complete assignments in all subject areas.

The first skill is recognizing organization. Through these activities, the student is made aware of relationships among ideas in a passage. Recognizing the organization of a reading passage provides structure and logic for the student. The ability to distinguish the main idea from supporting details, causes from effects, similarities from differences, and fact from opinion improves comprehension. In addition, recognizing sequence, drawing conclusions, and understanding analogies help develop thinking skills.

Adjusting reading rate enables students to locate information quickly or to analyze material in more depth. Recognizing when to use these strategies helps students use their time more efficiently.

Content area reading material uses a wide variety of graphic aids to support and develop concepts. Being able to derive information from these sources extends student comprehension. Graphic aids can clarify, reinforce, enrich, or teach, as well as provide a visual representation that benefits many students' learning patterns. The activities in this section offer ways to make graphic aids an integral part of the reading process.

The unit ends with a section on developing vocabulary. Some activities use structural analysis to have students examine word parts and then recognize meanings of the word parts in unfamiliar words. Further activities focus on context clues and multiple meaning words with specialized definitions.

All the activities in Unit I support the development of good reading skills, with the goal of having students carry these skills to the content area classroom.

SKILL A. Recognizing Organization

OBJECTIVE

Students will complete a variety of activities to help them develop their understanding of main idea, supporting details, sequence, cause/effect, fact/opinion, drawing conclusions, comparison/contrast, and analogies.

STRATEGIES

1. After students have learned to recognize an organizational pattern, you should reinforce their understanding of the pattern when it appears in classroom readings.

2. Many of the activities are easily adapted to your own classroom materials to reinforce the skills being developed. Use these activities often to help your students master each strategy taught.

SPECIAL DIRECTIONS

1. **"Giving Support to an Idea"**: You may choose to assign any or all of the extensions as additional assignments.

2. **"Getting the Main Idea I"**: Instead of having students write the key words and phrases on separate paper, they may use a highlighter marker instead.

TEACHING HINTS

Many of the activities in this section include techniques that are easily adapted to almost any reading material. You may wish to develop a worksheet to suit your own purposes and that may be used in any number of situations.

ANSWERS

IA-1 Getting the Main Idea I
2. storms; cause a good deal of damage; without warning; by strong winds and much rain

3. Students' answers may vary. Have students explain their reasoning for different responses. Here is a sample answer: Without much warning, storms can cause much damage with their heavy winds and rains.

IA-2 Getting the Main Idea II
2. not easy; early start; long walk/ride; change classes; many tasks; not simple; still not over; trip or homework

3. Being a student is not an easy job.

IA-6 Map It
2. Topic—transportation vehicles; Kinds—childhood vehicles, motorized vehicles, city mass transit, the airplane, space rockets

3. A sample semantic map:

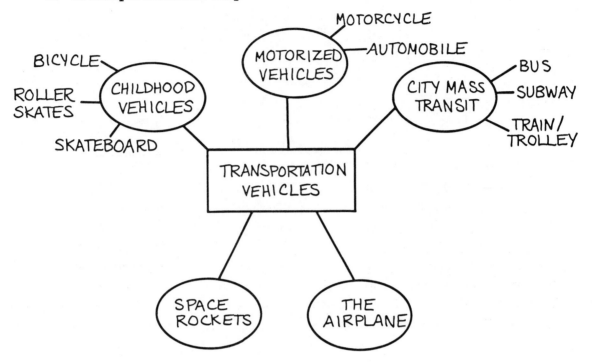

IA-7 *What's the Category?*
Have students explain reasons for their ways of ordering the elements within a category.

1. supplies—paper clips, pencils, pens, tape
2. cards—birthday, charge, library, playing
3. furniture—chair, couch, desk, dresser
4. fabric—cotton, linen, silk, wool
5. power source—battery, engine, sun, wind
6. jewelry—bracelet, earrings, pin, ring
7. soups—chicken, tomato, turkey, vegetable
8. coin—penny, nickel, dime, quarter
9. vehicle—bicycle, skateboard, parachute, plane
10. roads—avenues, boulevards, courts, highways

IA-8 *Giving Support to an Idea*
It is important to discuss the variety of student responses. Even more important, it is critical to have the students explain their rationales for their responses.

IA-10 What's the Order?
(1) Man sits down at table in restaurant; (2) Waiter gives him a menu; (3) Man orders and points to "chef's surprise"; (4) Chef tiptoes over behind man; (5) Chef yells "BOO" as man jumps.

IA-12 Sequencing a Story's Parts
1, 3, 6, 4, 5, 2

IA-22 Proving and Disproving Inferences
1. True. "Mom, I made it."/Scott recounted every detail . . .
2. False. . . . throwing his raincoat onto its hook . . .
3. True. Mrs. Reed hugged Scott and smiled./She said proudly . . .
4. True. "Mom, I made it."
5. True. "Mom, I made it."/Scott recounted every detail/the hours of practicing at the net in the driveway had paid off . . .

IA-23 Which Product to Purchase?
Car 1—8 miles per gallon; $185 maintenance for 3 months; extras are air conditioning, AM/FM radio and tape deck, fancy wheels, recliner seats; attractive sportscar; seats 2, tiny trunk space

    Car 2—15 miles per gallon; $200 maintenance for 6 months; extras are air conditioning, AM/FM radio, power windows/steering/brakes, anti-theft alarm; family station wagon; seats 7, large cargo area

IA-24 Is It an Alligator or a Crocodile?
    Similarities—both lay eggs, both are reptiles, both are coldblooded with scaly skin, both breathe with lungs.

    Differences—alligator is bigger; crocodile has long triangular head; alligator has wide flat head with broad round nose; crocodiles lay eggs in a hole in the ground; alligators build nests above ground.

IA-25 Finding the Similarities and Differences
Students' answers may vary. Discuss their rationale for the order they suggest. Categories will be physical characteristics, behavior, food, physical movement, defense, etc.

IA-26 How Similar?/How Different?
Have students explain their reasoning behind their similarities and differences.

IA-27 Analogies I
Accept responses which convey the same meaning as the answers below.

1. back
2. dark or heavy
3. down
4. tree
5. animal of any 2 or 4 legged type
6. eight
7. zipper or buttons or snaps

IA-28 Analogies II
Accept responses which convey the same meaning as the answers below.

1. dog
2. painter
3. fruit or tree
4. farmer
5. screw

6. dig
7. Texas
8. hand
9. chop
10. time

IA-29 Analogies III
Accept responses which convey the same meaning as the answers below.

1. dog
2. bird
3. dark or heavy
4. obese

5. baseball
6. scale
7. winter
8. trot

GETTING THE MAIN IDEA I

OBJECTIVE: Determining the main idea of a passage by asking key questions

PROCEDURE: Here is a strategy to help you determine the main idea of a passage. This strategy can be helpful for finding the main idea of many different kinds of reading selections. It can be used for short as well as long passages.

1.   Read the following passage:

STORMS!

Have you ever seen "The Wizard of Oz?" If so, then you have probably observed the power of the tornado, a wind storm that can cause a vast amount of damage. Tornados have been known to lift houses off of their foundations and cars right off the highways. The tornado is only one example of how nature can cause destruction. Hurricanes, too, have been known to cause their share of damage. These storms have tremendous winds and with the winds comes a vast amount of rain. Flooding often results from a hurricane. This leaves people stranded in their homes or cars and often without power. These are but two types of storms which affect us, often with little advance warning.

2.   Answer the following questions. Remember that it is not always possible to answer all of the questions from the information given in a short passage. In such a case, just leave a question unanswered.

Who or what is the passage about?

_____

What happened?

_____

When?

_____

Where?

_____

How?

_____

Why?

_____

3.   Using your answers to the preceding questions, write a one-sentence statement that captures the main idea of the passage.

_____

_____

EXTENSION: Find a newspaper or magazine passage to read. Then use a marker to highlight the answers to the various questions in number 2 above.

GETTING THE MAIN IDEA II

OBJECTIVE: Determining the main idea of a passage by using key words and phrases

PROCEDURE: This strategy will help you to determine the main idea of a passage. In this strategy you will focus on the key word or phrase in each sentence of a passage.

1.   Read the following short passage:

> Being a student is not always an easy job. For example, it requires an early start in the day. Often it involves a long walk or bus ride. Once at school, the student moves from class to class. In each class he or she must perform a variety of tasks: reading, writing, and listening. Often the tasks are not simple. Once three o'clock comes, it is still not over. There is the trip home, homework, and planning for yet another day of school.

2.   Notice that there are eight sentences in this passage. Let's first identify the topic of this passage. Then, find a key word or phrase from each sentence which contributes some idea to the overall topic. Two sentences have been done as examples.

Topic: being a student

Sentence 1:   not easy _____

Sentence 2:   early start _____

Sentence 3:   _____

Sentence 4:   _____

Sentence 5:   _____

Sentence 6:   _____

Sentence 7:   _____

Sentence 8:   _____

3.   Now examine the topic and your list of key words and phrases. What do these key words and phrases help us to know about this topic? Write your response in one sentence. Your sentence may include some of the key words and phrases if they help you to state the main idea of the passage.

Main Idea: _____

_____

_____

A MAIN IDEA COLLAGE

OBJECTIVE: Creating a picture or word collage to suggest a particular main idea
MATERIALS: For this activity, you will need poster paper, colored drawing pens or pencils, magazines and newspapers, scissors, and glue.
PROCEDURE:

1. Select a theme, characteristic, or emotion to portray through a collage of words or pictures.
2. Decide whether you want to use a collage of words or pictures to portray this idea.
3. Locate pictures or words from magazines and newspapers that will help you to communicate this idea.
4. Arrange these pictures or words on your poster paper to form an attractive presentation.
5. On the back of your presentation, print the main idea you have illustrated.
6. Share your collage with the class and see if they can determine the main idea that it communicates.

A MAIN IDEA CHART

OBJECTIVE: Creating a chart to show the key ideas presented within a passage

PROCEDURE: It is often possible to present the main ideas and supporting details of a reading selection in a chart form. Such a chart often helps to clarify the main points within a given reading.

1. Read the following passage:

   In the English language there are eight main parts of speech. First, there is the noun. The noun names people, places, things, and ideas. Second, there is the pronoun. The pronoun is used to take the place of the noun. Both the noun and the pronoun name things. In addition, there are parts of speech whose main function is to describe. The adjective is a word which describes a noun or a pronoun. The adverb describes adjectives, verbs, or other adverbs. The verb, a necessary sentence part, tells something about the subject of the sentence. There are three other parts of speech. The preposition shows a relationship between two nouns or pronouns. The conjunction is used to connect words, phrases, or sentence parts. Finally, there is the interjection whose main purpose is to show strong emotion. Each part of speech has its own function.

2. This reading passage helps to explain what is meant by the eight parts of speech. The passage identifies each part of speech and the purpose of each. Here is one way to chart this information.

PART OF SPEECH	FUNCTION	EXAMPLE

A MAIN IDEA CHART (continued)

3. After your "Parts of Speech Chart" is complete, try to construct a more creative graphic showing this information. For example, a chart showing the reasons for many Europeans coming to America could include a map of the European continent, the Atlantic Ocean, and the American mainland. Then the reasons for coming could be written on arrows which would appear to be pushing a boat toward America. Or, if you were explaining the parts of a fish's body, you could draw a fish and actually include the information about each body part near the actual part. Use color to finish the graphics.

4. Select a passage from one of your textbooks and design a graphic to communicate the main ideas of the selection.

Name _____   Date _____

WRITING A HEADLINE

OBJECTIVE: Creating a headline to state the main idea of a news article

MATERIALS: For this activity you will need a newspaper and scissors.

PROCEDURE:

1. Locate an interesting article in your newspaper. The article should be one that you think your classmates would enjoy reading.
2. Cut out the article, then cut off the headline to the article.
3. Bring your news article to class and share it with them.
4. Have members of the class share their ideas for a good headline for the article.
5. Have each student who suggests a specific headline give his or her reasons for the suggestion. The details of the article should support each choice.

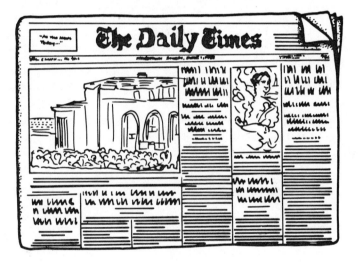

MAP IT

OBJECTIVE: Constructing a semantic map to organize the information within a reading passage

MATERIALS: For this activity you will need a pencil, straight edge, colored drawing pens or pencils, and paper.

PROCEDURE: This strategy is designed to help you remember the details in a reading passage and organize them in a meaningful way.

1. Read the following passage:

   There are a variety of transportation vehicles in our world, each having its own purpose. From our childhood days, we know that the bicycle, roller skates, and skateboard helped us get around town. As we got older, we quickly came to know the convenience of motorized vehicles like the motorcycle and automobile. Those of us who lived in city areas are also familiar with the bus, subway, and trolley. These help to move many people at the same time. If we want to travel far distances in a short time, we might take advantage of the airplane. Some humans have also traveled to space in rockets. Indeed, many transportation vehicles have been developed over the years.

2. After reading this passage, consider the important points. Record your ideas below.

   Topic: _____

   Kinds of Transportation Vehicles:
   — childhood vehicles

   — motorized vehicles

   — _____

   — _____

   — _____

3. You can now draw a semantic or word map to help show the main ideas and supporting details of this paragraph following the directions on the next page of this activity.

Name _____ **Date** _____

MAP IT (continued)

PROCEDURE (cont.)

    a.   Place the topic of the paragraph in the center block of the following diagram.

    b.   On each line that comes off this block, put a type of vehicle.

    c.   Off each type of vehicle, draw some additional lines on which you can list examples of that type of vehicle.

Note: If you wish, use a different color for each category of vehicles. This sometimes helps to make the ideas clearer.

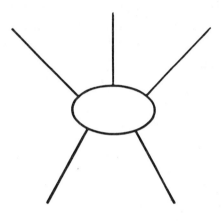

A Sample Semantic Map

    Here is a semantic map for the topic My Pet Collie:

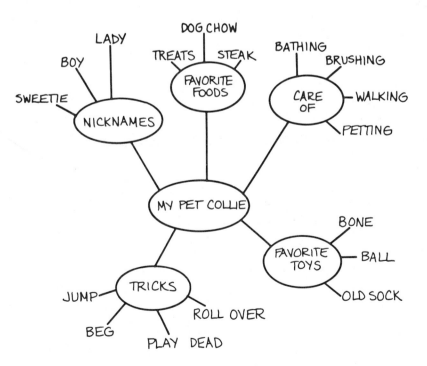

WHAT'S THE CATEGORY?

OBJECTIVE: Distinguishing a category label from its members

MATERIALS: For this activity, you will need a pencil.

PROCEDURE:

1. Study each group of words.

2. Decide which word is the category word.

3. Place this word on the top line.

4. Then place the words in this category underneath the category label. If there is a logical order in which to list these words, list them that way. This order may be alphabetical, time order, biggest to smallest, most important to least important, etc.

EXAMPLE: Alabama   states   New Jersey   Maine   California

states _____
        Alabama
        California
        Maine
        New Jersey

1. pens   pencils   paper clips   supplies   tape

    _____

        _____

        _____

        _____

        _____

2. library   playing   cards   charge   birthday

    _____

        _____

        _____

        _____

        _____

WHAT'S THE CATEGORY? (continued)

3. couch   furniture   chair   dresser   desk

_____

_____

_____

_____

_____

4. silk   wool   fabric   cotton   linen

_____

_____

_____

_____

_____

5. battery   engine   sun   wind   power source

_____

_____

_____

_____

6. bracelet   earrings   jewelry   ring   pin

_____

_____

_____

_____

_____

WHAT'S THE CATEGORY? (continued)

7. tomato   chicken   turkey   soups   vegetable

_____

      _____

      _____

      _____

      _____

8. quarter   coin   dime   nickel   penny

_____

      _____

      _____

      _____

      _____

9. skateboard   parachute   plane   bicycle   vehicle

_____

      _____

      _____

      _____

      _____

10. highways   roads   avenues   courts   boulevards

_____

      _____

      _____

      _____

      _____

EXTENSION: Create some original lists like those above. Exchange your lists with a classmate and categorize each list.

GIVING SUPPORT TO AN IDEA

OBJECTIVE: Writing sentences to support a topic sentence
MATERIALS: For this activity, you will need a pencil.
PROCEDURE: Below you will find some sentences with three lines underneath each. On these lines, write three sentences to support this first sentence. These sentences could be details, reasons, examples, etc.

1. Going to the beach on the weekend is great fun.

    a. _____

    b. _____

    c. _____

2. Having a part-time job has its advantages.

    a. _____

    b. _____

    c. _____

3. Computers have certainly changed our lives.

    a. _____

    b. _____

    c. _____

4. The games of tennis and ping-pong are similar in some ways.

    a. _____

    b. _____

    c. _____

5. There are many different ways to relax on the weekend.

    a. _____

    b. _____

    c. _____

GIVING SUPPORT TO AN IDEA (continued)

6. It certainly is fun to eat out.

    a. _____

    b. _____

    c. _____

7. There are many responsibilities to being a parent.

    a. _____

    b. _____

    c. _____

8. There are certain qualities that I look for in a good friend.

    a. _____

    b. _____

    c. _____

9. Being lost can be a frightening experience.

    a. _____

    b. _____

    c. _____

10. I have always enjoyed reading a good mystery story.

    a. _____

    b. _____

    c. _____

EXTENSION 1: Create some original topic sentences like those above. Exchange with a classmate and fill in the supporting details.

EXTENSION 2: Create some original supporting details. Have a classmate write a topic sentence that summarizes the supporting details.

EXTENSION 3: Select one of the topic sentences and supporting details. Write a paragraph using the information. Feel free to add additional details as needed.

HOW MUCH DO WE KNOW?

OBJECTIVE: Categorizing a listing of brainstormed ideas from the class

MATERIALS: For this activity, you will need pencil and paper.

PROCEDURE:

1.   On a sheet of paper write a list of five ideas you have about sharks.

2.   Share your ideas with the class. As each student shares ideas, add to your list those ideas that you did not have.

3.   Once you have your list of ideas, group those ideas together that have something in common. Give each category a label.

4.   Do this until all ideas are in a category. It might be necessary to eliminate some ideas that don't seem to fit in with the other ideas.

5.   Decide upon a logical order to arrange these categories. Then arrange each idea within each category.

6.   Share your ideas with the class.

EXTENSION: Use this organization of ideas to write a short summary of the class's ideas on sharks. Each category could be a separate paragraph. Use the category label to develop a topic sentence.

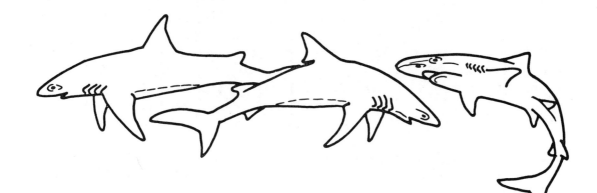

WHAT'S THE ORDER?

OBJECTIVE: Sequencing the frames of a comic strip into a logical order
MATERIALS: For this activity, you will need scissors.
PROCEDURE:
1.   Cut out the pictures below.
2.   Arrange the pictures in a logical order.
3.   Be prepared to share which clues in each picture helped you to decide upon the order.

CREATING A TIMELINE

OBJECTIVE: Creating a timeline for a fictional character in a story

MATERIALS: For this activity, you will need poster paper, colored pencils or drawing pens, and a ruler.

PROCEDURE:

1. Look at the sample timeline. Important events in the life of the person are shown.
2. Choose a character from a story you have read.
3. List some things that happened to the character.
4. Put these events into chronological order.
5. Make a time line to show the events in order.
6. You may want to illustrate events on the time line with pictures.

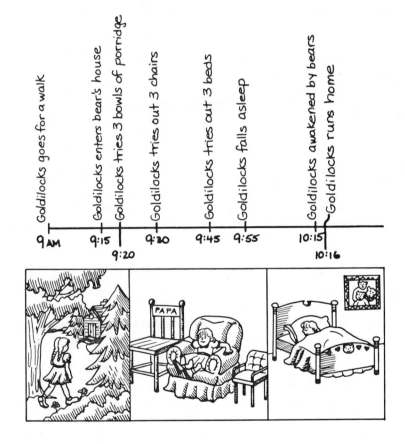

SEQUENCING A STORY'S PARTS

OBJECTIVE: Arranging the paragraphs of a story into a logical order
MATERIALS: For this activity, you will need a pencil.
PROCEDURE: Read the paragraphs below and determine the correct order of the paragraphs. Place a number beside each paragraph to show the sequence.

_____   Joe woke with a start. Then he heard the wind beating the rain against his window. As he lay still in bed, he noticed the sound of his own breathing. He began to fall asleep when he heard a distant noise. He sat up to listen. Then he heard it again.

_____   This time Joe was sure the sound came from downstairs. He slowly walked out of his bedroom into the hall. He froze on the stairs as he heard it again. His mind raced as he tried to imagine what it was. His thoughts jumped from robbers to monsters to ghosts to aliens from outer space.

_____   Joe opened the door and pulled the screen door tight. He secured the latch and closed the door with a sigh of relief. He laughed at his imagined ghosts and went back to bed.

_____   Should he get out of bed and investigate? Was it just the storm or house noises? He got out of bed and tiptoed to the door.

_____   In a few seconds he would reach the kitchen. What would he find there? Slowly he reached for the door. He opened it and felt along the wall for the light switch. He could feel his heart beating. He flipped on the lights just as he heard a bang. He ran to the back door to discover that the screen door was not caught in the latch. The door creaked again as the wind blew it open. Then it slammed with a bang.

_____   The house was so quiet as he peered into the darkness from his bedroom. He strained to listen. Rain, wind, and a barking dog could be heard outside. But Joe was sure he had heard a sound inside the house. Suddenly, he heard it again!

"Cartooning" a Story

OBJECTIVE: Showing the sequence of events in a story through a comic strip

MATERIALS: For this activity, you will need colored pencils or drawing pens, poster paper, and a ruler.

PROCEDURE: Read the following story. Then show the story in a comic strip. Use your drawings, rather than words, to communicate.

Heidi and her brother Gary were excited. Today, they were going to the pound to get a dog. They had wanted one for a long time, and, finally, Mom had agreed.

Heidi and Gary looked through the cages at many dogs. Then they both ran over to a very shaggy, large, clumsy puppy. He licked them and jumped up excitedly as they became acquainted.

In the car on the way home, the two children happily held the large puppy and began trying to name him. He was a mixed breed and difficult to identify. This gave Heidi an idea. "I know. Let's call him U.F.O. because he's our own Unidentified Furry Object!"

EXTENSION: Write your own story and then show it through a comic strip.

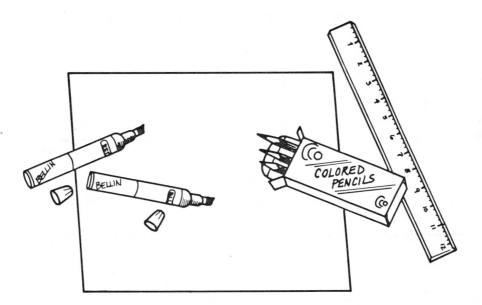

WHAT IF?

OBJECTIVE: Hypothesizing effects from a specific cause
MATERIALS: For this activity, you will need a pencil.
PROCEDURE:

1. Choose a famous event, such as the invention of the airplane.
2. In the chart below, list ways in which the world was affected by the event.
3. Imagine that the event never occurred or that a different event took place.
4. Then list all the ways you can think of that the world would have been different if the imagined event had really taken place.

Actual Event: _____
Effects on the World:

    1. _____

    2. _____

    3. _____

    4. _____

    5. _____

Imagined Event: _____
Effects on the World:

    1. _____

    2. _____

    3. _____

    4. _____

    5. _____

Name _____ Date _____

CAUSE-EFFECTS-SOLUTIONS

OBJECTIVE: Identifying possible effects for a particular cause and hypothesizing solutions for the problems created

MATERIALS: For this activity, you will need a pencil.

PROCEDURE:

1. Imagine a problem situation, such as growing to be ten feet tall or scientists predicting that the world will end in ten days.
2. In the chart below, list some effects the problem situation might cause.
3. Then list ways to solve each of the problems listed.

Event: _____

POSSIBLE EFFECTS	POSSIBLE SOLUTIONS
1.	
2.	
3.	
4.	

EXTENSION: Draw the possible effects and solutions.

IA-15

CAUSES AND EFFECTS

OBJECTIVE: Identifying causes and effects

MATERIALS: For this activity, you will need a pencil.

PROCEDURE:

1. Choose an event, such as raising the speed limit on highways, getting a new puppy, or earning good grades on your report card.
2. On the chart below, write in the event. Then fill in the factors that caused the event to take place.
3. Then fill in the effects the event might cause.

Event: _____

CAUSES OF THE EVENT	EFFECTS OF THIS EVENT
1.	
2.	
3.	
4.	
5.	

Name ______________________________ Date ______________

I. READING SKILLS | *A. Recognizing Organization* | *4. Cause/Effect*

LEARNING OF AN EVENT'S CAUSES AND EFFECTS

OBJECTIVE: Conducting library research to identify the causes and effects of a particular event

MATERIALS: For this activity, you will need reference books and a pencil.

PROCEDURE:

1. Choose an historical event, such as people landing on the moon, and write it on the chart below. Do some research to find out what caused the event to occur and what effects happened as a result of the event.
2. Fill in the events that caused the event to happen.
3. Then fill in some of the effects caused by the event chosen event.

Event: ______________________________

CAUSES OF THE EVENT	EFFECTS OF THE EVENT
1.	
2.	
3.	
4.	
5.	

EXTENSION: Make a diagram to show the relationship among the elements on the chart.

Name _____ Date _____

FACT OR OPINION?

OBJECTIVE:　Identifying facts and opinions

MATERIALS:　For this activity, you will need a pencil.

PROCEDURE:　A fact is a statement that can be proved. Opinions, however, are your personal thoughts based on feeling. Choose a controversial question, such as "How much homework should students have?" or "Are girls smarter than boys?" List at least ten facts and ten opinions about the question. Use the back of this sheet to continue your list.

Question: _____

FACTS	OPINIONS
1.	
2.	
3.	
4.	

(Continue on other side.)

IA-18

DISTINGUISHING FACTS FROM OPINIONS

OBJECTIVE: Stating and identifying facts and opinions

MATERIALS: For this activity, you will need a pencil, colored pencils, a newspaper editorial, and paper.

PROCEDURE:

1. Cut out a newspaper editorial to read.
2. Use one colored pencil to underline all the facts.
3. Use another colored pencil to underline all the opinions.
4. Write your opinion as a newspaper editorial about whether schools should be open twelve months a year.
5. Use one colored pencil to underline all the facts in your editorial.
6. Use another colored pencil to underline all the opinions in your editorial.

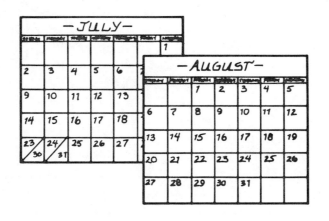

Name _____ Date _____

SUPPORTING AN OPINION

OBJECTIVE: Supporting an opinion with information gathered through library research

MATERIALS: For this activity, you will need reference books, a pencil, and paper.

PROCEDURE:

1. Choose a controversial question such as "Should animals be used for medical research?"
2. Write a statement explaining your opinion about the topic.
3. Read at least two magazine articles from the library that discuss the chosen topic.
4. Revise your opinion statement if necessary.
5. Write an explanation supporting your opinion. Use facts from your research in your writing.

FINISHING A STORY

OBJECTIVE: Drawing conclusions to complete a story

MATERIALS: For this activity, you will need a pencil.

PROCEDURE: Read the following story. Then, on the back of this sheet, write your own ending. Take into consideration the logical flow of events and the likelihood of your ending.

John and Sara rowed far out onto the lake. John wanted to be sure no one else would overhear them. He had thought long and hard before reaching his difficult decision. Now that he had decided to tell Sara his secret, he wanted to do it with no interruptions.

John and Sara were both counselors at Camp Winnihopat. For John, the summer job was a way to earn money he needed for college, and it provided an escape from home. Things at home had become unbearable with his father's drinking. The arguing, the fighting, the tears, and the anger were more than John could handle. That was why he had lied about being able to swim. He desperately wanted and needed this summer job. Now he was responsible for watching little kids swim in the lake and he didn't know how to swim himself.

Sara was a real friend, but would she understand? Would she turn him in? Would she think of a way out of this mess? He would soon find out. Sara sat silently as John blurted it all out.

When John had finished telling Sara his secret, . . .

PROVING AND DISPROVING INFERENCES

OBJECTIVE: Identifying evidence from a passage to check the validity of inferences

MATERIALS: For this activity, you will need a pencil.

PROCEDURE: Read the passage. For each inference, use the chart to give evidence from the passage to prove or disprove the statement.

Scott raced into the house, throwing his dripping raincoat onto its hook and leaving his boots on the mat. "Mom, I made it!"

Mrs. Reed hugged Scott and smiled. "Tell me all about it," she said proudly.

Scott recounted every detail of his tryout for the varsity team, including his hook shot, his lay up, and his free throws. The hours of practicing at the net in the driveway had paid off.

INFERENCE	AGREE/DISAGREE	EVIDENCE FROM PASSAGE
1. Scott was happy.	____ ____	
2. It was a sunny day.	____ ____	
3. Mrs. Reed was glad for Scott.	____ ____	
4. Scott was Mrs. Reed's son.	____ ____	
5. Scott liked basketball.	____ ____	

Name _____ Date _____

WHICH PRODUCT TO PURCHASE?

OBJECTIVE: Comparing two products and then drawing conclusions about which product to purchase

MATERIALS: For this activity, you will need a pencil and "Which Product to Purchase" handout.

PROCEDURE: Fill in the chart based on information from the two ads. Decide which product you would buy and, on the back of this sheet, explain why.

CONSIDERATIONS	CAR 1	CAR 2
Miles per gallon		
Maintenance cost		
Extras		
Attractiveness		
Carrying capacity		

Name —————— Date ——————

WHICH PRODUCT TO PURCHASE? (continued)

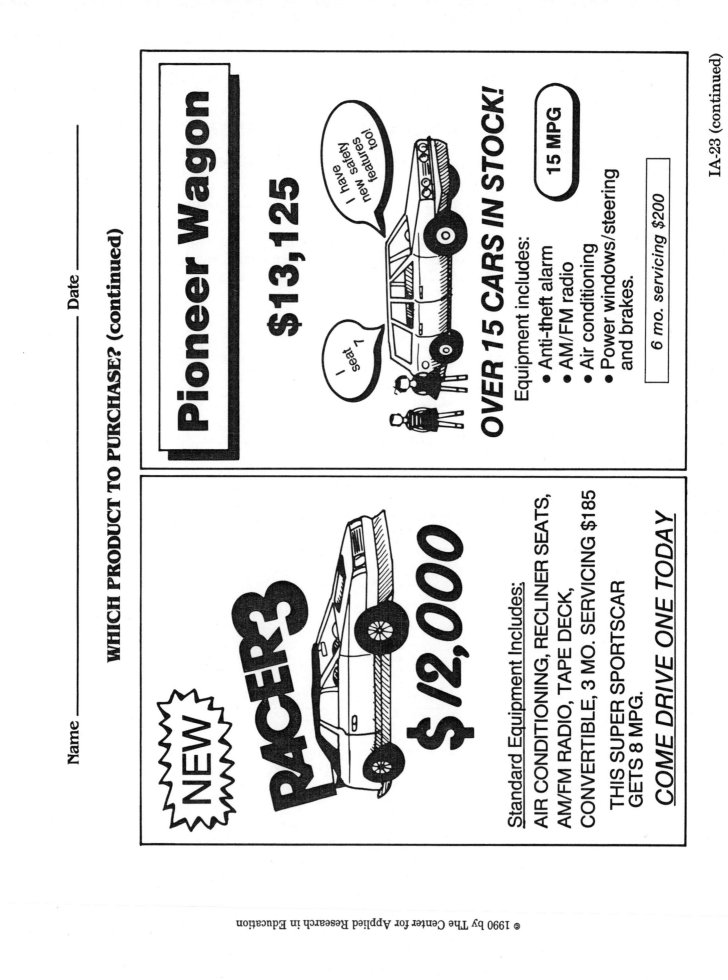

IS IT AN ALLIGATOR OR A CROCODILE?

OBJECTIVE: Identifying similarities and differences between alligators and crocodiles

MATERIALS: For this activity, you will need a pencil.

PROCEDURE: Read the passage. Then, on the back of this sheet, make a chart to list similarities and differences between alligators and crocodiles.

Do you know the difference between alligators and crocodiles? Alligators are the world's largest reptiles. They are cold-blooded with scaly skin, they lay eggs, and they breathe with lungs. The easiest way to tell alligators and crocodiles apart is by their heads. Crocodiles have long, triangular heads, while alligators have wide, flat heads with broad, round noses.

Another way to tell them apart is by their nests. Most crocodiles dig a hole in the ground into which they lay their eggs. Alligators, on the other hand, build their nests above ground by using mounds of leaves, branches, and mud.

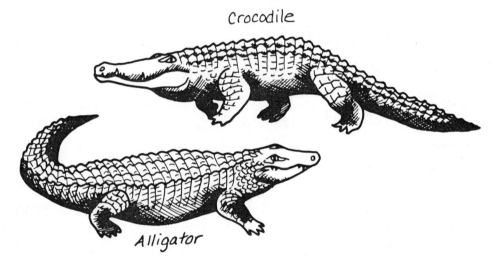

Crocodile

Alligator

EXTENSION: Choose two similar things to contrast. Write a list of the differences between the two things. Then use your notes to write an explanation of the differences between the two.

FINDING THE SIMILARITIES AND DIFFERENCES

OBJECTIVE: Identify the similarities and differences within a list of statements and organizing them

MATERIALS: For this activity, you will need a pencil, scissors, paper, and paste.

PROCEDURE: Cut out each statement below. Arrange the statements into groups based on similarities and differences. Then paste the statements to another sheet of paper to form paragraphs.

Giraffes are the tallest animals.

They have the same number of vertebrae (seven) in their necks as do humans.

Giraffes are partially color blind.

They confuse green, orange, and yellow.

The name *giraffe* comes from an Arab word meaning "the one that walks very fast."

Giraffes have very weak vocal cords and an underdeveloped larynx, resulting in a very weak voice.

Giraffes can usually outrun their attackers.

While searching for food, a giraffe may walk hundreds of miles in a few months.

A walking giraffe takes stides about fifteen feet long.

Giraffes can make a variety of sounds including grunts, snorts, whistles, and growls.

As giraffes eat, they watch for enemies, such as lions.

Giraffes generally stay away from places where they can't see lions.

When a lion is seen, a giraffe will begin running.

Giraffes display affection by pressing their necks together.

I. READING SKILLS   *A. Recognizing Organization*   *7. Comparison/Contrast*

HOW SIMILAR?/HOW DIFFERENT?

OBJECTIVE: Identifying similarities and differences among a group of words

MATERIALS: For this activity, you will need a pencil.

PROCEDURE: Read each group of words. Then identify and write the similarities and differences among the words in the group.

1. BIG – LITTLE – HUGE – GARGANTUAN – SMALL – TINY

    similarities: _____

    differences: _____

2. RED – FLAME – RUBY – ROSE – SCARLET

    similarities: _____

    differences: _____

3. KIND – GENTLE – FRIENDLY – GENEROUS

    similarities: _____

    differences: _____

4. SHOWER – SPRINKLE – STORM

    similarities: _____

    differences: _____

5. PROPEL – PROMOTE – PROJECT – PROLONG

    similarities: _____

    differences: _____

6. AGILE – AWKWARD – NIMBLE – CLUMSY

    similarities: _____

    differences: _____

I. READING SKILLS   *A. Recognizing Organization*   *8. Analogies*

ANALOGIES I

OBJECTIVE: Identifying relationships among words

MATERIALS: For this activity, you will need a pencil.

BACKGROUND: An analogy is a statement that shows the relationship between pairs of words. Some analogies use ideas that are opposites. For example: BIG is to LITTLE as WET is to DRY. Some analogies show a part-to-whole relationship. For example: FINGER is to HAND as TOE is to FOOT.

HINT: It is helpful to develop a sentence that shows the relationship between the first pair of words. Then try and insert the second pair to see if the relationship is the same. For example: BIG is the opposite of LITTLE, and WET is the opposite of DRY. A FINGER is a part of the HAND, and a TOE is a part of a FOOT.

PROCEDURE: Read the completed pair of words and look for a relationship between the two words. (Try to apply the hint mentioned above.) Then read the first word of the second pair. (Remember that it is like the first word in the first pair.) Try to think of a word to make the second pair of words similar in their relationship to the completed pair of words. (Again, remember the hint.)

1. RIGHT is to LEFT as FRONT is to _____.

2. DAY is to NIGHT as LIGHT is to _____.

3. HOT is to COLD and UP is to _____.

4. STEM is to PLANT as TRUNK is to _____.

5. WING is to BIRD as LEG is to _____.

6. TEN is to FORTY as TWO is to _____.

7. SHOELACE is to SHOE as _____ is to JACKET.

EXTENSION 1: Make up some original analogies that are either opposite in relationship or part-to-whole in relationship.

EXTENSION 2: Illustrate some of the above analogies, showing the relationship between the words.

EXTENSION 3: Illustrate some original analogies.

© 1990 by The Center for Applied Research in Education

I. *READING SKILLS*   *A. Recognizing Organization*   *8. Analogies*

ANALOGIES II

OBJECTIVE: Identifying relationships among words

MATERIALS: For this activity, you will need a pencil.

BACKGROUND: An analogy is a statement that shows the relationship between pairs of words. Some analogies use ideas that show an example and category relationship. For example: CARDINAL is to BIRD as DOG is to MAMMAL. Some analogies show a tool and worker relationship, or a tool and use relationship. For example: PEN is to WRITE as POT is to CHEF.

HINT: It is helpful to develop a sentence that shows the relationship between the first pair of words. Then try and insert the second pair to see if the relationship is the same.

PROCEDURE: Read the completed pair of words and look for a relationship between the two words. (Try to apply the hint mentioned above.) Then read the first word of the second pair. (Remember that it is like the first word in the first pair.) Try to think of a word to make the second pair of words similar in their relationship to the completed pair of words. (Again, remember the hint.)

1.   ANGORA is to CAT as TERRIER is to _____.

2.   SAW is to CARPENTER as PAINTBRUSH is to _____.

3.   TULIP is to FLOWER as APPLE is to _____.

4.   NEEDLE is to TAILOR as PLOW is to _____.

5.   HAMMER is to NAIL as SCREWDRIVER is to _____.

6.   KNIFE is to CUT as SHOVEL is to _____.

7.   BOSTON is to MASSACHUSETTS as DALLAS is to _____.

8.   SNEAKER is to FOOT as GLOVE is to _____.

9.   BROOM is to SWEEP as AX is to _____.

10.   THERMOMETER is to TEMPERATURE as CLOCK is to _____.

EXTENSION: Create some original analogies that have an example of category relationship or a tool and worker relationship or a tool and use relationship. You may want to illustrate your analogies, too.

ANALOGIES III

OBJECTIVE: Identifying relationships among words

MATERIALS: For this activity, you will need a pencil.

BACKGROUND: Analogies show relationships between pairs of words. Analogies can show many kinds of relationships, such as part to whole, synonyms, opposites, child-adult, cause and effect, and many others.

PROCEDURE: Read the completed pair of words in each analogy and determine the relationship between the words. Then find a word to complete the second pair that uses the same relationship.

HINT: It is helpful to develop a sentence that shows the relationship between the first pair of words. Then try and insert the second pair to see if the relationship is the same.

1. CALF is to COW as PUPPY is to _____.

2. MEOW is to CAT as TWEET is to _____.

3. GOOD is to BAD as LIGHT is to _____.

4. SLIM is to THIN as FAT is to _____.

5. RACKET is to TENNIS as BAT is to _____.

6. INCH is to RULER as POUND is to _____.

7. DAY is to NIGHT as SUMMER is to _____.

8. SNAKE is to SLITHER as HORSE is to _____.

EXTENSION: Create some of your own analogies. Trade them with a classmate and try to solve them.

© 1990 by The Center for Applied Research in Education

SKILL: B. Adjusting Reading Rate

OBJECTIVE:
Students will complete a variety of activities designed to improve reading efficiency.

STRATEGIES:
1. Prior to assigning a particular reading to your students, you can help the student by setting a purpose for the reading. For example, you might ask students to read to find out the decision a main character makes, the differences and similarities between two items, or the causes of a particular event.

2. Before students read a passage, have them use text headings and graphics to predict what the passage will be about and what information they may find.

3. It will help students to show them that there are different degrees of reading. One can scan a passage for a specific piece of information, one can skim a passage to get an overall idea of the reading, and one can read much more thoroughly for appreciation of an author's description or for detailed instructions. Helping the students to see the importance of the varied degrees of reading and when each one may be useful is important.

4. Discuss with students those factors that might affect the speed at which a student will read a specific passage:
   - level of familiarity with content of reading
   - what the students will have to do with the material once it has been read
   - amount of time available for reading
   - level of vocabulary
   - complexity of sentence structure

5. These activities for adjusting reading rate can be applied to all classroom textbook assignments to reinforce the skill.

TEACHING HINTS:
1. **"Getting the Idea":** After the students have completed the activity, have them read the textbook chapter. Then help students analyze their summaries and predictions, focusing on the accuracy of their understanding after only five minutes of reading.

2. **"Order, Order":** After the students have completed the activity, discuss (as a group) the reasoning behind the various organizations. Help the students see how some pieces of information are related to each other.

3. **"First Things First":** After this activity, have the students read the chapter carefully to evaluate the accuracy of their summaries.

ANSWERS:

IB-3 Order, Order
Accept any reasonable response. Have students explain their reasoning for the order they have selected.

IB-6 Can You Find the Information?
1. a planet
2. Auroran people discovered Earth
3. Sent Auroran researchers to Earth to investigate
4. to find out how people on Earth communicated, learned and traveled
5. two years
6. television
7. Rora, Wynda, Ari
8. on the North American continent
9. bicycles, skateboards, surfboards, planes, automobiles

IB-7 It's a Matter of Time
1524—Verrazano is first European to enter New York Harbor
1609—Henry Hudson reaches Manhattan and sails up Hudson River named for him
1613—Adriaen Block becomes first European to settle Manhattan
1614—Block and these Europeans leave Manhattan
1626—Dutch West India Company sends settlers to Manhattan who set up town and build Fort Amsterdam
1647—Peter Stuyvesant becomes governor of New Amsterdam
1664—English take New Amsterdam by force and make Dutch surrender

Name _____ Date _____

WHAT'S IT ALL ABOUT?

OBJECTIVE: Using a chapter's headings and subheadings to predict a chapter's contents

MATERIALS: For this activity, you will need a pencil and paper.

PROCEDURE: (1) The headings and subheadings below are arranged in the order in which they were found in a textbook chapter. As you read them carefully, think about what the chapter might discuss. (2) Next, make some notes on the outline about each section. The basis for your notes may come from television, movies, books, and people you know. Write everything that comes to mind on each topic, including opinions and impressions. (3) Using your notes, write a paragraph on the "History of the Automobile," a paragraph on the "Changes in the Automobile," and a paragraph on "American Lifestyles."

Chapter Title: The Automobile in America
  I.   History of the Automobile
      A.   Inventor of the Automobile
      B.   The First Cars
      C.   Cars Cause Problems in Early Days

  II. Changes in the Automobile
      A.   Body Styling from Early Days to Present
      B.   Materials for Building Cars
      C.   Influence of Foreign Car Builders

 III. The Car's Influence on American Lifestyles
      A.   The Drive-in Movie
      B.   Growth of the Suburbs
      C.   Easy Banking and Easy Eating

EXTENSION: Select a chapter in one of your textbooks. Use the headings and subheadings to write a short summary in which you predict the contents of the chapter.

Name _____   Date _____

GETTING THE IDEA

OBJECTIVE: Skimming a chapter for an overview
MATERIALS: For this activity, you will need a pencil, paper, and textbook chapter.
PROCEDURE:

1. Open your textbook to the chapter assigned to you by your teacher.

2. For five minutes, skim the chapter in order to learn the subject of the chapter and to get an idea of the points made by the author. Focus on headings and subheadings to get a general idea of each section. Read quickly through the text without reading every single word.

3. Once your five minutes are up, close the textbook. Write an opening sentence to a paragraph in which you state the subject/topic of the chapter. Then write some supporting sentences that suggest what other information the author presents on this topic. Write here:

_____

_____

_____

_____

4. Following this paragraph, write some questions you predict will be answered in the chapter. Use the space below for your questions. If you need more space to write, use another sheet of paper.

_____

_____

_____

_____

_____

_____

_____

_____

ORDER, ORDER

OBJECTIVE: Organizing headings and subheadings for a given chapter

MATERIALS: For this activity, you will need paper, a pencil, scissors, and tape.

PROCEDURE: (1) Below you will find a listing of headings and subheadings for a textbook chapter. Cut out each heading and subheading. (2) Arrange these strips into a logical order. Look for categories that will be your main headings and then find the subheadings that will go under the headings. (3) Once you have them in an order, tape them onto a sheet of paper. Share your order with your classmates.

Chapter 1: Our Weather
Barometers and Air Pressure
Tools of the Meteorologist
Hurricanes
Windvanes and the Wind
Satellites Assist the Weather Forecasters
Snow, Hail, and Sleet Storms
Many Kinds of Weather Conditions
How the Weather Affects Us
Tornados
People's Moods
Destruction of Property
Injuries and Deaths

EXTENSION: Write down on individual slips of paper each heading and subheading from an upcoming chapter in one of your textbooks. Have a classmate arrange these slips into a logical order.

Name _____ Date _____

FIRST THINGS FIRST

OBJECTIVE: Previewing a reading passage by reading only the first sentence of each paragraph

MATERIALS: For this activity, you will need a textbook passage, paper, and a pencil.

PROCEDURE:

1. In this activity, you will learn a strategy that can help you gain an overview of a specific reading passage. This activity is not designed to be used when reading for detailed information; it is a strategy that is useful for getting a general idea of a passage and for reviewing information you have already read.

2. Open your textbook to the specific chapter assigned by your teacher.

3. Read the first sentence in each paragraph of the chapter. As you do this, think of how each sentence relates to the one you have read before and predict what the upcoming sentence will talk about.

4. Once you have finished, write a short summary that states the chapter topic and subtopics. Use the space below. If you need more space to write, use another sheet of paper.

_____

_____

_____

_____

_____

_____

_____

_____

_____

_____

_____

GRAPHIC AIDS AS HINTS TO A CHAPTER'S CONTENTS

OBJECTIVE: Using graphic aids within a chapter to get an overview of the chapter's content

MATERIALS: For this activity, you will need a textbook chapter containing a variety of graphic aids, a pencil, and "Graphic Aid Preview of a Chapter."

PROCEDURE:

1. In this activity, you will use only the pictures, graphs, charts, maps, cartoons, and other graphic aids in the chapter assigned by your teacher. For each graphic aid in the chapter, fill in the requested information on your copy of "Graphic Aid Preview of a Chapter." For example:

TEXTBOOK PAGE	TYPE OF GRAPHIC AID	TOPIC OF GRAPHIC AID	MAIN IDEA OF GRAPHIC AID
37	Map	Routes of explorers	The explorers had dangerous routes.
39	Picture	Sick sailors	Many sailors on ships became sick.

2. Write a paragraph in which you predict what the chapter will be about. In your topic sentence, state what you believe the subject of the entire paragraph will be. Then develop the paragraph by mentioning other key points as shown through the graphic aids. If you need more space to write, use the back of this sheet.

_____

_____

_____

_____

_____

_____

_____

_____

GRAPHIC AID PREVIEW OF A CHAPTER

TEXTBOOK PAGE	TYPE OF GRAPHIC AID	TOPIC OF GRAPHIC AID	MAIN IDEA OF GRAPHIC AID

CAN YOU FIND THE INFORMATION?

OBJECTIVE: Scanning a reading passage for specific information

MATERIALS: For this activity, you will need "Aurora Reading Passage," a pencil, and a highlighter marker.

PROCEDURE: (1) Below you will find a set of questions that you will be asked to answer. However, instead of reading the passage completely, you will be asked to scan the passage quickly looking only for the answers. Your eyes should cue in on key words, dates, places, names, etc., from the questions. (2) Read the questions. Using your highlighter, go over those key words from the questions that give a hint as to what to look for. (3) Now scan the passage for the answer to each question. Use your highlighter to mark those words that answer the questions. (4) Share your answers with your classmates.

Questions to Be Answered Based Upon Reading Passage:

1. What is Aurora?

_____

2. What happened on the date of August of 2021?

_____

3. As a result of this discovery, what did the leaders of Aurora do?

_____

4. What was the purpose of this mission?

_____

5. For how long was this visit supposed to be?

_____

6. What was the square box the researchers mentioned?

_____

7. Who were the three researchers sent to Earth?

_____

8. Where on Earth did they land?

_____

9. What were two forms of travel they saw?

_____

AURORA READING PASSAGE

In August of 2021, the citizens of the planet Aurora were thrilled with their new interplanetary discovery: Earth. For years, they had an idea that other people existed in the Universe. While on an exploratory mission, the commanders of the Spaceship Cintar discovered the planet.

Following this discovery, the Auroran leaders sent a team of researchers to Earth to investigate the planet. They were sent to find out how the people of Earth communicated, learned, and traveled. The researchers would spend two years on the planet.

Upon arrival, Rora, Wynda, and Ari settled on the North American continent. They observed that people communicated both with some kinds of sounds and through hand motions. There also was a square box that seemed to have an unlimited number of people inside of it.

The people on Earth seemed to spend a great deal of time in schools. They would read, write, calculate math problems, exercise, and construct things. There was usually someone in front of the room doing a lot of talking.

Travel seemed to be not only a necessity for the people of Earth but also a form of recreation. People traveled on two-wheeled vehicles, long boards on top of waves, in birdlike vehicles, and a rather creative invention called the automobile.

The Auroran researchers returned to their planet at the conclusion of the two years and reported back to their leaders about the Earth people. They were certainly fascinated with the information and would soon push for a meeting with the Earth citizens to establish friendly relations between the two planets.

IT'S A MATTER OF TIME

OBJECTIVE: Skimming a reading selection for dates

MATERIALS: For this activity, you will need a pencil and "New York City Reading Passage."

BACKGROUND: When reading certain selections, it is sometimes logical to focus on dates and what happened on those dates. At times, it will be efficient to list these dates in time order and indicate what happened on each date.

PROCEDURE: (1) Skim the reading passage. As you skim it, circle the dates mentioned. (2) Using the chart below, arrange these dates in order from the earliest to the latest in the left-hand column. In the right-hand column, write the event that happened on that date.

DATE	EVENT

New York City Reading Passage

New York City is the largest American city. Although the American Indians were the earliest known residents of the New York City area, it wasn't until 1524 that the first European explorer, Giovanni da Verrazano, entered New York Harbor. Later, in 1609, Henry Hudson reached Manhattan and sailed up the Hudson River which was named for him. He was an Englishman who sailed for the Netherlands. In 1613 a Dutch trader by the name of Adriaen Block and his crew became the first Europeans to settle on the island. They stayed until the spring of 1614. The Dutch West India Company, a trading company, sent over a group of settlers to the island of Manhattan. By 1626 these settlers set up a town and built Fort Amsterdam at the southern end of the island. Peter Minuit became the governor of the island and bought the island from the Indians for about twenty-four dollars worth of goods. The settlement became known as New Amsterdam. In 1647 Peter Stuyvesant became the governor of the settlement. Unfortunately for the Dutch, the English began to cause problems. They too wanted to settle in the area. In 1664 English warships sailed into the New York Harbor and made the Dutch surrender. Under English rule New Amsterdam became known as New York.

SKILL: C. Reading Graphic Aids

OBJECTIVE:

Students will complete a variety of activities to help them develop their skills in reading graphic aids.

STRATEGIES:

1. During regular classroom teaching, make students aware of the elements within pictures:
   - picture title or boldface heading
   - caption
   - clues within the picture: who? (person, animal, thing, relationships); what is happening? (context of the situation); when? (time clues); where? (geographic or spatial location); why or how? (cause/effect, comparison/contrast)

2. When text material includes diagrams, help students note and recognize these key elements:
   - title
   - operational clues (arrows, lines, numerical ordering, dotted lines, variations of print size, color and form, etc.)
   - arrangement of parts
   - key
   - vocabulary
   - labels
   - captions

3. Discuss with students the organization of tables in text materials and in the environment.

4. When reading a line or bar graph, discuss with students the data to be shown. Help students to conclude that the Y axis usually shows a scale of measurement; the X axis usually shows examples that have been measured. Point out that all graphs have a title and some may include a legend explaining features on the graph.

5. Review with students the elements of a map: symbols, legends, scale, and title.

6. Review with students the purposes of maps. Maps are representations of locations. They may show a variety of information including weather conditions, transportation routes, water bodies, land forms, and political regions.

SPECIAL DIRECTIONS:

1. **"How Much Can You Find?":** This activity works well in small groups as a cooperative learning activity. Have the groups also classify their observations.

2. **"Can You Find the Answer?":** Divide the class into small groups for this activity. Assign a different picture to each group. Pictures may come from texts, library books, posters, or any other available source.

3. **"What Does a Diagram Show?":** Point out to the students the relationships shown in the diagram. Make note of the sequences shown and the variety of sequences. Explain that a diagram can show more. Help the students conclude that some information can be given more efficiently in a diagram than in a narrative.

TEACHING HINTS:

Incorporate information presented in graphic aids into classroom discussions and quizzes. The inclusion of these materials makes students aware of their value in text material.

ANSWERS:

IC-5 What Does a Diagram Show?
Accept all reasonable responses, including the following:

grass — grasshopper — fish — bear

grass — caterpillar — fish — frog — bear

grass — mouse — snake — hawk — bear

grass — bear

dragonfly — fish — bear

grass — mouse — hawk — bear

raccoon — bobcat — bear

IC-7 What's in a Bar Graph?
1. heights of boys in Mrs. Lowe's class
2. names of boys
3. number of inches
4. two; 65 inches
5. 70 inches; 52 inches
6. Answers will vary; however, each response must be proven through using data on the graph.

IC-8 What's in a Pictograph?
1. 100 cans
2. week 1; 200 cans
3. week 4; 600 cans
4. Answers will vary.
5. 250

IC-9 What's in a Line Graph?
1. average seasonal rainfall in Springfield
2. Summer; 14 days

3. Fall; 4 days

4. Winter and Spring

5. Summer and Fall

IC-10 What's in a Circle Graph?
1. how Rick spends his allowance

2. food

3. food 40%; clothes 25%; movies, tapes and videos 20%; school supplies 10%; miscellaneous 5%

IC-11 What's on a Map?
Answers will vary.

IC-12 What's in a Map Legend?
1. ✈

2. 1

3. a. ⊢⟜⊣   b. —⬭—   c. ⌂

4. Washington Monument, Lincoln Memorial, Jefferson Memorial

5. bridge

IC-13 What's on a Road Map?
1. Newtown

2. 30 miles

3. Route 46

4. west

5. Country Mile Road

IC-14 How High Is It?
1. over 5,000 feet

2. 0–1000 feet

3. Ghost Hill, Alligator Alley, and Cypress

4. 1001–2000 feet

IC-15 Where Is It?
Boston—Suffolk—MA—New England—USA—NA
Atlanta—Fulton—GA—South—USA—NA
Miami—Dade—FL—South—USA—NA
Chicago—Cook—IL—Midwest—USA—NA
Los Angeles—Los Angeles—CA—West—USA—NA
Phoenix—Maricopa—AZ—Southwest—USA—NA
Seattle—King—WA—West—USA—NA
Philadelphia—Philadelphia—PA—Northeast—USA—NA
Dallas—Dallas—TX—Southwest—USA—NA
Denver—Denver—CO—Rocky Mountain States—USA—NA

HOW MUCH CAN YOU FIND?

OBJECTIVE:　Reading a picture

MATERIALS:　For this activity, you will need a pencil and paper.

PROCEDURE:　Look at the picture. Then, for five minutes, list all the observations you can make about this picture. Share your observations with the rest of the class.

WHAT'S IN A PICTURE?

OBJECTIVE: Reading a picture
MATERIALS: For this activity, you will need a picture from a textbook and a pencil.
PROCEDURE: People say that a picture is worth a thousand words. Find a picture in your textbook. Look carefully at the picture. There is often much information in a picture that is overlooked. The information may be directly observed or it may be inferred from observable clues. Use your textbook picture to complete as much of this chart as possible.

Title of Picture: _____
Who is in the picture?

    people: _____

    animals: _____

    objects: _____
What is happening?

    past occurrences: _____

    present happenings: _____

    future possibilities: _____
When is it?
    time of day: _____   clues to support: _____

    season: _____   clues to support: _____

    historical
    time period: _____   clues to support: _____
Where is it?

    climate: _____

    land characteristics: _____

    water characteristics: _____

WHAT'S IN A PICTURE? (continued)

clothing: _____

vegetation: _____

housing structures: _____

transportation: _____

How/Why?
Write two statements about the picture that explain the "how" or "why" of any observed phenomenon.

Statement 1: _____

_____

Statement 2: _____

_____

Vocabulary

Word	Speculated Definition
_____	_____
_____	_____
_____	_____

Question
Write one question you would like to have answered about this picture.

Question: _____

_____

Name _____ Date _____

WHAT'S IN THE CHAPTER?

OBJECTIVE: Reading pictures and captions to get an overview of a textbook chapter

MATERIALS: For this activity, you will need a textbook and a pencil.

PROCEDURE: Turn to the next chapter you will study in your textbook. Use only the pictures and their captions to answer the following questions.

Book title: _____

Chapter title: _____

Pages: _____ to _____

1. What things will you study in this chapter?

_____

_____

2. What are some facts contained in the pictures and the captions?

_____

_____

3. What are some questions you believe will be answered in the chapter?

_____

_____

4. What are some vocabulary terms significant to the topic of this chapter?

_____

_____

CAN YOU FIND THE ANSWER?

OBJECTIVE: Reading a picture
MATERIALS: For this activity, you will need a picture and a pencil.
PROCEDURE: (1) Carefully observe a picture. (2) Write five questions that can be answered by looking at the picture. (3) Exchange pictures and questions with other students. Answer the new set of questions. (4) Share your answers with the authors of the questions.

QUESTIONS	ANSWERS
1. _____	1. _____
_____	_____
_____	_____
2. _____	2. _____
_____	_____
_____	_____
3. _____	3. _____
_____	_____
_____	_____
4. _____	4. _____
_____	_____
_____	_____
5. _____	5. _____
_____	_____
_____	_____

WHAT DOES A DIAGRAM SHOW?

OBJECTIVE: Reading a diagram

MATERIALS: For this activity, you will need a pencil and paper.

PROCEDURE: (1) Look at the diagram. The arrows show the movement of energy through organisms in a food web. (2) Choose one animal from the top level of the food web. List the path through which energy passed before reaching your animal. Then list a different path for the same animal. (3) Write a paragraph explaining the diagram. Use words that indicate sequence, such as first, then, at the same time, after, last, etc.

FOOD WEB DIAGRAM

WHAT'S IN A GRAPH?

OBJECTIVE: Reading bar graphs, line graphs, and pictographs
PROCEDURE: Read about each type of graph.

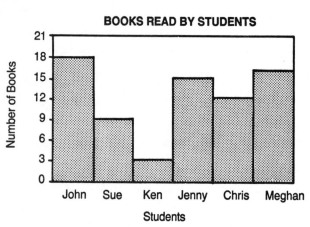

BAR GRAPH: A bar shows data on a bar graph.

Follow the top of each bar over to the scale to find the number the bar represents.

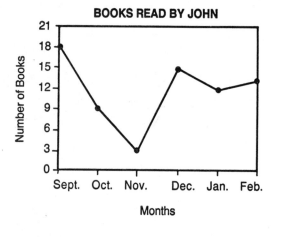

LINE GRAPH: A line connects points on a line graph to show change.

Follow each point over to the scale to find the number the point represents.

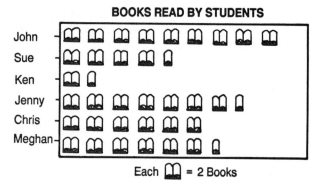

PICTOGRAPH: Symbols represent numbers on a pictograph.

Count the symbols to compute the data.

Comparisons are easily seen on a bar graph and a pictograph.

Name _____ Date _____

WHAT'S IN A BAR GRAPH?

OBJECTIVE: Reading a bar graph
MATERIALS: For this activity, you will need a pencil.
PROCEDURE: Use this graph to answer the questions.

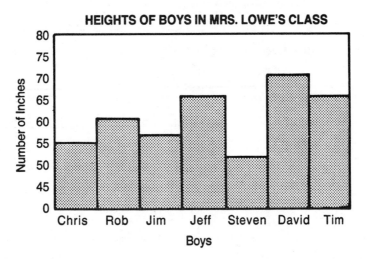

1. What does the bar graph show?

   _____

2. What characteristic is shown on the X axis (along the bottom of the graph)?

   _____

3. What characteristic is shown on the Y axis (along the left side of the graph)?

   _____

4. How many boys are the same height? _____ What is the height? _____

5. What is the tallest height? _____ What is the shortest height? _____

6. What conclusion can you make based on the graph?

   _____

   _____

   _____

WHAT'S IN A PICTOGRAPH?

OBJECTIVE: Reading a picture graph
MATERIALS: For this activity, you will need a pencil.
PROCEDURE: Use this pictograph to answer the questions.

ALUMINUM CANS RECYCLED

Week 1
Week 2
Week 3
Week 4
Week 5
Week 6

Each ⬜ =100 Cans

1. What does ⬜ mean?

    _____

2. During which week were the fewest cans recycled? How many?

    _____

3. During which week were the most cans recycled? How many?

    _____

4. Why might one week have more cans recycled than the other weeks?

    _____

5. How many cans were recycled during Week 3?

    _____

© 1990 by The Center for Applied Research in Education

Name _____ Date _____

WHAT'S IN A LINE GRAPH?

OBJECTIVE: Reading a line graph
MATERIALS: For this activity, you will need a pencil.
PROCEDURE: Use this line graph to answer the questions.

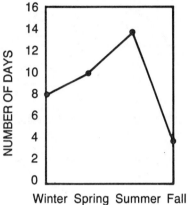

1. What does the graph show?

_____

2. Which season has the most rain? How many days?

_____

3. Which season has the least rain? How many days?

_____

4. Between which seasons is there the least change?

_____

5. Between which seasons is there the greatest change?

_____

EXTENSION: Use the back of this sheet to summarize the information in a paragraph. The first sentence of the paragraph should give the main idea of the graph. The sentences that follow should give conclusions supported by detailed information from the graph.

WHAT'S IN A CIRCLE GRAPH?

OBJECTIVE: Reading a circle graph
MATERIALS: For this activity, you will need a pencil.
PROCEDURE: Use this circle graph to answer the questions.

HOW RICK SPENDS HIS ALLOWANCE

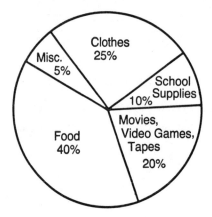

1. What does the graph show?

    _____

2. Which category on the graph shows the greatest amount spent?

    _____

3. List the categories and their percentages from the greatest to the least.

    _____

    _____

    _____

    _____

    _____

© 1990 by The Center for Applied Research in Education

WHAT'S ON A MAP?

OBJECTIVE: Reading a map

MATERIALS: For this activity, you will need a pencil and the "What's on a Map?" handout.

PROCEDURE: Study the two maps on the handout. Then answer the questions below.

How are these two maps the same? _____

_____

_____

_____

_____

_____

_____

_____

How are these two maps different? _____

_____

_____

_____

_____

_____

_____

_____

WHAT'S ON A MAP? (continued)

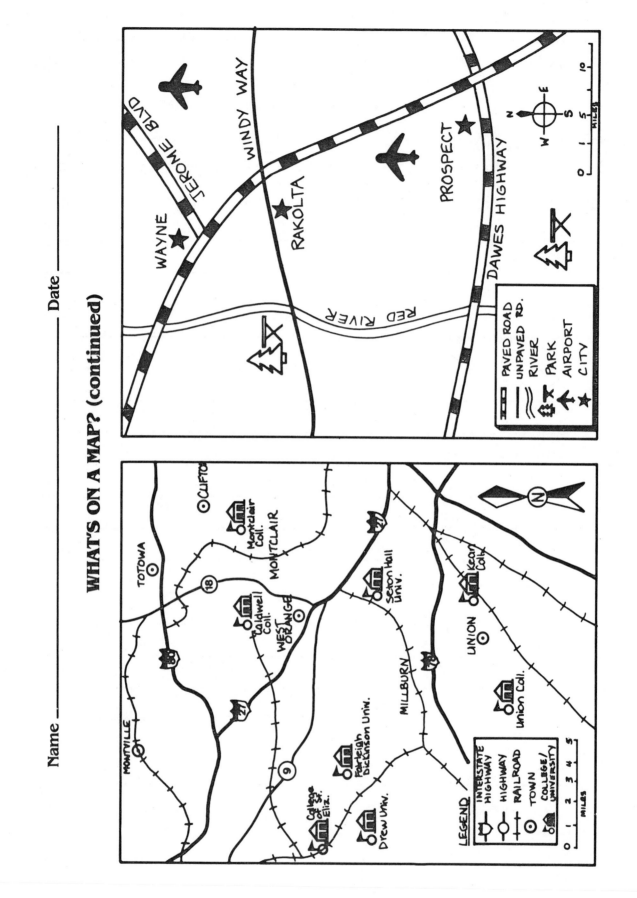

WHAT'S IN A MAP LEGEND?

OBJECTIVE: Reading a legend on a map

MATERIALS: For this activity, you will need the "What's in a Map Legend?" handout and a pencil.

PROCEDURE: Use the map legend on the handout to answer the questions.

1.   What is the symbol for an airport?

_____

2.   How many airports are shown on the map?

_____

3.   What symbols are used to show the following?

a.   U.S. Highway _____

b.   State Highway _____

c.   U.S. National Monument _____

4.   What national monuments are shown on the map?

_____

_____

_____

_____

_____

5.   What does this ⋈ show?

_____

_____

WHAT'S IN A MAP LEGEND? (continued)

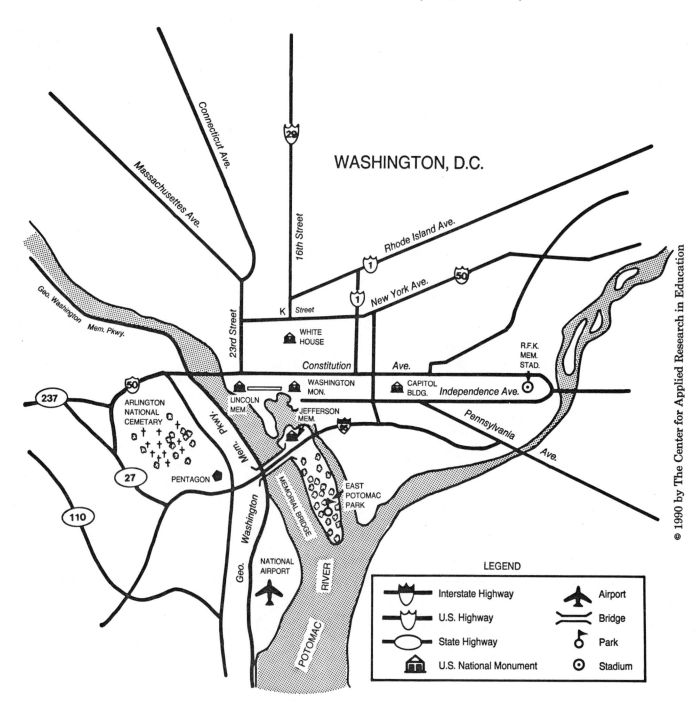

WASHINGTON, D.C.

LEGEND

⚑ Interstate Highway		✈	Airport
⚑ U.S. Highway		≍	Bridge
⬭ State Highway		⚲	Park
🏛 U.S. National Monument		⊙	Stadium

WHAT'S ON A ROAD MAP?

OBJECTIVE: Reading a road map
MATERIALS: For this activity, you will need a pencil.
PROCEDURE: Use this map to answer the questions.

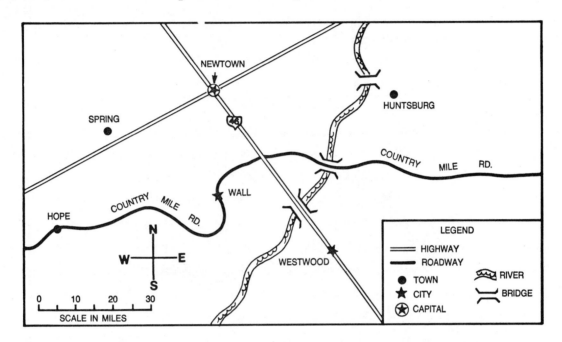

1. What town is directly north of Wall?

_____

2. How far is it from Spring to Newtown?

_____

3. What highway goes from Newtown to Westwood?

_____

4. From Huntsburg, in which direction must you travel to reach Newtown?

_____

5. On which road would you travel from Hope to Wall?

_____

Name _____ Date _____

HOW HIGH IS IT?

OBJECTIVE: Reading an elevation map

MATERIALS: For this activity, you will need a pencil.

PROCEDURE: An elevation map tells about the height of land. Look at the legend to find how many feet above sea level each shaded area on the map is. Each shade shows a range of elevation that can include hills, valleys, and mountains.

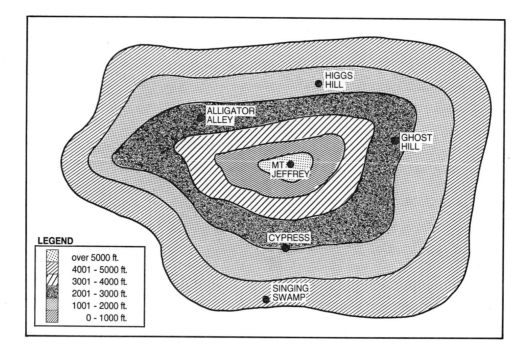

1. What is the elevation of Mt. Jeffrey?

   _____

2. What is the elevation of Singing Swamp?

   _____

3. What towns have an elevation of 2000 to 3000 feet?

   _____

4. What is the elevation of Higg's Hill?

   _____

WHERE IS IT?

OBJECTIVE: Locating places on a map
MATERIALS: For this activity, you will need reference books and a pencil.
PROCEDURE: Use maps in your social studies textbooks, atlases, geography books, or library reference books to complete the chart below.

CITY/TOWN	COUNTY	STATE	REGION	COUNTRY	CONTINENT
Boston					
Atlanta					
Miami					
Chicago					
Los Angeles					
Phoenix					
Seattle					
Philadelphia					
Dallas					
Denver					

SKILL: D. Developing Vocabulary

OBJECTIVE:
Students will complete a variety of activities to help in the development of vocabulary.

STRATEGIES:
1. Point out to students the importance of vocabulary in the content areas and help them take responsibility for improving their understanding of these words.

2. Many activities teach strategies for developing vocabulary. Encourage students to use these strategies and reinforce them whenever possible.

3. When a new word is encountered in the classroom, provide a model for students in how to determine the word's meaning. Verbalize each step your mind goes through as you attempt to determine the meaning. For example, consider this statement and the underlined word:

    The explorer descended into the <u>subterranean</u> cavern. You might say, "Subterranean? What clues do I have about this word's meaning? I know 'sub' means 'under,' and it says that the explorer descended which means the explorer went down . . ." etc.

4. Have students create original crossword puzzles using word parts.

ANSWERS:

ID-1 What Does It Mean?
1. autobiography: a person's life story by him- or herself
2. biology: study of life
3. export: something carried out or from a place
4. geology: study of earth
5. geography: study of earth's surface
6. import: to carry in or into
7. invisible: not seen
8. report: to carry back
9. telegraph: to write far
10. telephone: to send a voice or sound far
11. television: to send a picture far
12. transport: to carry across

ID-2 How Do Word Parts Affect the Meaning of Words?
1. move—to move
2. script—written
3. vis—see
4. micro—very small
5. sub—below
6. path—feeling

ID-4 *Getting the Meaning*

1. translocation: the process of carrying across
2. transpiration: the process of respiration in a plant
3. xerophytes: dry plants
4. hydrophytes: water plants
5. mesophytes: plants on the land
6. halophytes: salt-loving plants

ID-6 *In Context*

1. organisms: living things
2. food chains: steps through which energy is transferred
3. producers: plants that store energy from the sun in their tissue
4. consumers: organisms that eat plants or other consumers for energy
5. herbivores: consumers that only eat plants
6. carnivores: consumers that only eat animals
7. omnivores: consumers that eat both plants and animals
8. decomposers: organisms that feed on the decaying tissue of dead producers and consumers

ID-7 *Guessing the Word*

1. show
2. indicate or show
3. shed
4. get rid of
5. tearing
6. eaten
7. real

ID-10 *What's an Idiom?*

1. try to begin again
2. just making it
3. wash one's body
4. she's nervous
5. lose one's temper
6. becoming hysterical
7. very hungry
8. very happy
9. depressed
10. lost one's temper

Name _____ Date _____

WHAT DOES IT MEAN?

OBJECTIVE: Determining the meaning of unfamiliar words using structural analysis
MATERIALS: For this activity, you will need a pencil.
PROCEDURE: Knowing the meanings of some word parts can help you understand the meanings of words you may not know. Use the table of word parts and their meanings to determine the meanings of the words below.

Common Word Parts and Meanings			
Word Part	*Meaning*	*Word Part*	*Meaning*
auto	self	phone	sound, voice
bio	life	port	carry
ex	out, from	post	after
geo	earth	pre	before
graph	write	re	back
im, in	in, into, not	tele	far
inter, intra	between	trans	across
logy	study of	vid, vis	to see

1. autobiography: _____

2. biology: _____

3. export: _____

4. geology: _____

5. geography: _____

6. import: _____

7. invisible: _____

8. report: _____

9. telegraph: _____

10. telephone: _____

11. television: _____

12. transport: _____

HOW DO WORD PARTS AFFECT THE MEANING OF WORDS?

OBJECTIVE: Identifying the meaning of a word part after defining several words containing the same word part

MATERIALS: For this activity, you will need a pencil.

PROCEDURE: Write the definitions for the following words. Then try to identify the meaning of the word part for each group.

1.   a. movable: _____

   b. movement: _____

   c. mover: _____

   d. immovable: _____

   word part: _____ *meaning:* _____

2.   a. transcript: _____

   b. inscription: _____

   c. manuscript: _____

   d. script: _____

   word part: _____ *meaning:* _____

3.   a. video: _____

   b. vision: _____

   c. visible: _____

   d. visit: _____

   word part: _____ *meaning:* _____

4.   a. microscope: _____

   b. microphone: _____

   c. microorganism: _____

   d. microrecorder: _____

   word part: _____ *meaning:* _____

HOW DO WORD PARTS AFFECT THE MEANING OF WORDS?
(continued)

5. a. subscript: _____

    b. submarine: _____

    c. subterranean: _____

    d. submit: _____

    word part: _____ *meaning:* _____

6. a. empathy: _____

    b. sympathy: _____

    c. pathetic: _____

    d. pathology: _____

    word part: _____ *meaning:* _____

HOW MANY WORDS FROM ONE PART?

OBJECTIVE: Expanding vocabulary by finding and defining
                       words containing a given word part

MATERIALS: For this activity, you will need a pencil.

PROCEDURE: Complete the chart for a word part, such as
                       "tri."

Word part:	Definition:
WORDS CONTAINING THE WORD PART	DEFINITIONS

Name _____ Date _____

GETTING THE MEANING

OBJECTIVE: Drawing meaning for unfamiliar terms by using structural analysis
MATERIALS: For this activity, you will need a pencil.
PROCEDURE: Read the passage. Then try to define each underlined word by using the list of word parts and meanings.

Word Part	*Meaning*
halo	salt
hydro	water
locus	place
meso	in the middle
phyte	plant
spirare	breathe
trans	across
xero	dry

Plants need water to produce food, to transport materials, and to provide support. Plants use water to carry the materials needed for life. Materials dissolved in water are carried throughout the plant in a process called <u>translocation</u>. Water vapor escapes from plants through the process of <u>transpiration</u>.

Plants have adapted to the scarcity or abundance of water. <u>Xerophytes</u>, such as cacti, are able to grow in places where water is scarce, while <u>hydrophytes</u>, such as duckweed, are able to live in or near water. Most familiar land plants, such as oak trees, are <u>mesophytes</u>. <u>Halophytes</u>, such as aloe, have adapted to live in salty soils.

© 1990 by The Center for Applied Research in Education

1. translocation: _____

    _____

2. transpiration: _____

    _____

3. xerophytes: _____

    _____

4. hydrophytes: _____

    _____

5. mesophytes: _____

    _____

6. halophytes: _____

    _____

IS IT A WORD?

OBJECTIVE: Using prefixes and suffixes to form words

MATERIALS: For this activity, you will need a pencil.

PROCEDURE: (1) Use the lists of prefixes and suffixes to form words with a common root. (2) Write the words and their definitions on the lines below. Be sure your definitions distinguish similar words. Use the back of this sheet if you need more space to write.

Prefixes	*Roots*	*Suffixes*
in, im	aud	ion
de	avi	sion
dis	cred	ance, ence
re	duc, duct	ment
pre, pro	mov, mot	ness
post	scrib, script	able, ible
trans		ive
sub		ish
com, con		ary

——

——

——

——

——

——

——

——

——

——

——

Name _____ Date _____

IN CONTEXT

OBJECTIVE: Using context clues to define words in a passage
MATERIALS: For this activity, you will need a pencil.
PROCEDURE: Read the passage. Then define each underlined word by focusing on the way each word is used in the passage. Clues to the meanings of words are given within the paragraph. An appositive, a phrase set off by commas, often gives the definition or an example of the word before the first comma.

Organisms, or living things, depend on the sun for energy. Almost all food chains, the steps through which energy is transferred, begin with the sun. Producers, or plants, store energy from the sun in their tissues. Then consumers eat producers or other consumers to obtain energy. Herbivores, such as rabbits, are consumers that feed on plants only. Carnivores, such as wolves, feed on other animals. Omnivores, such as bears, feed on both plants and animals. Decomposers, such as fungi, feed on producers and consumers by breaking down the tissues of dead organisms. Through food chains, energy is passed from one organism to another.

1. organisms: _____

   _____

2. food chains: _____

   _____

3. producers: _____

   _____

4. consumers: _____

   _____

5. herbivores: _____

   _____

6. carnivores: _____

   _____

7. omnivores: _____

   _____

8. decomposers: _____

   _____

GUESSING THE WORD

OBJECTIVE: Using context clues to derive meaning for deleted words in a passage
MATERIALS: For this activity, you will need a pencil.
PROCEDURE: Read the entire passage. Then go back and write words or phrases in the blanks to complete the paragraph.

Humans cry to (1) _____ their feelings. Our tears may

(2) _____ sadness, anger, or happiness. But why do crocodiles cry?

Crocodiles' eyes (3) _____ tears, just as ours do. Scientists believe

that the tears help the crocodile (4) _____ excess salt from its body.

Humans get rid of extra salt through sweating.

There is a legend about how the saying "crocodile tears" began. The legend says

that the crocodile would cry, (5) _____ and moaning and

pretending to be very sad. Anyone or anything who came to see what was wrong would

quickly be (6) _____ by the hungry crocodile. Today, the phrase

"crocodile tears" means tears that are not (7) _____ .

DETECTING WORD MEANINGS

OBJECTIVE: Using context to detect the meanings of words with multiple meanings
MATERIALS: For this activity, you will need a pencil.
PROCEDURE: Read each group of sentences. Then, in your own words, write a definition to show the meaning of each underlined word.

1. Jodi looked very sad, so I tried to find out what was the matter.

    _____

    In science class, we learned that matter is anything that has mass and takes up space.

    _____

2. An object's mass refers to the amount of matter in the object.

    _____

    On Sunday we went to mass at church.

    _____

    The rain turned the papers into a mass of soggy pulp.

    _____

3. My Aunt Martha plays the organ while my cousins sing along.

    _____

    The stomach is an organ of digestion in the body.

    _____

4. Strawberry plants start new plants by growing runners.

    _____

    At the beginning of the race, the runners lined up.

    _____

DETECTING WORD MEANINGS (continued)

5. I have to practice <u>scales</u> on the piano.

_____

The tropical fish had brightly colored <u>scales</u>.

_____

I weighed the fruit on the balance <u>scale</u>.

_____

6. Muscle <u>tissue</u> is made up of cells that are able to shorten.

_____

When I had a cold, I seemed to always be in need of a <u>tissue</u>.

_____

MULTIPLE-MEANING WORDS

OBJECTIVE: Comparing sentences to illustrate the multiple meanings of words

MATERIALS: For this activity, you will need a pencil and perhaps a dictionary.

PROCEDURE: Write two sentences to show different meanings for each of the following words. Use a dictionary if needed.

1. form   a. _____

                b. _____

2. blue   a. _____

                b. _____

3. fire   a. _____

                b. _____

4. stock   a. _____

                b. _____

5. bark   a. _____

                b. _____

6. run   a. _____

                b. _____

7. pass   a. _____

                b. _____

8. light   a. _____

                b. _____

9. pick   a. _____

                b. _____

10. float   a. _____

                b. _____

MULTIPLE-MEANING WORDS (continued)

11. play   a. _____

              b. _____

12. sink   a. _____

              b. _____

13. show   a. _____

              b. _____

14. side   a. _____

              b. _____

15   row   a. _____

              b. _____

WHAT'S AN IDIOM?

OBJECTIVE: Understanding idioms
MATERIALS: For this activity, you will need a pencil and perhaps a dictionary.
PROCEDURE: An idiom is a phrase that has a special meaning different from the meaning of its individual words. Read the idioms below. Then write the meaning of each idiom. Use a dictionary if needed.

1. turn over a new leaf

_____

2. by the skin of his teeth

_____

3. take a shower

_____

4. butterflies in her stomach

_____

5. fly off the handle

_____

6. laughed her head off

_____

7. could eat a horse

_____

8. tickled pink

_____

9. down in the dumps

_____

10. hit the roof

_____

HAVING FUN WITH PUNS

OBJECTIVE: Inventing original puns using words with multiple meanings
MATERIALS: For this activity, you will need a pencil.
PROCEDURE: A pun is a play on words that uses or misuses a word in a humorous way. Read the puns below and analyze why they are funny. Underline the word-play and explain what the two meanings are.

What do you call lions born in Chicago? **Chicago Cubs**

_____

_____

What do ants order on pizza? **ANT-chovies**

_____

_____

What is a cow's favorite game? **MOO-nopoly**

_____

_____

What did the crowd say when the pterosaur took off? **"Watch that dino soar!"**

_____

_____

EXTENSION: Try to think of some original puns. Think of words with multiple meanings or words that sound like other words. Then try to use the words in a humorous way.

I. READING SKILLS   *D. Developing Vocabulary*   *3. Multiple Meanings*

HOW ARE WORDS RELATED?

OBJECTIVE: Using semantic mapping to see relationships between words
MATERIALS: For this activity, you will need a pencil and scrap paper.
PROCEDURE: (1) Write a word in the center box of the word map below. (2) On scrap paper, write all the words you can think of that are related to the center word. (3) Put all the words in categories. (4) Write the words by category in the boxes around the center word. (5) You may need to add more boxes and connecting lines.

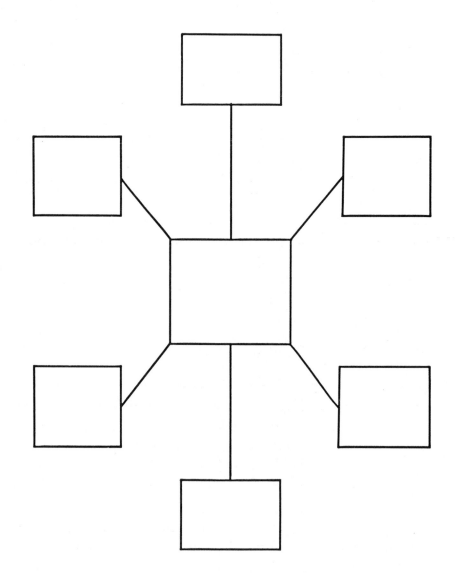

HOW ARE SYNONYMS DIFFERENT?

OBJECTIVE: Recognizing semantic differences among synonyms

MATERIALS: For this activity, you will need a pencil.

PROCEDURE: (1) Title the chart with a word that describes a category. (2) Under the column titled "Words," list some words within the category. (3) Write characteristics of some of the words in the spaces across the top of the chart. (4) Shade in the square next to each word under the characteristics that apply. (5) Analyze how each word is similar to and different from the other words in the chart.

WORD: _____

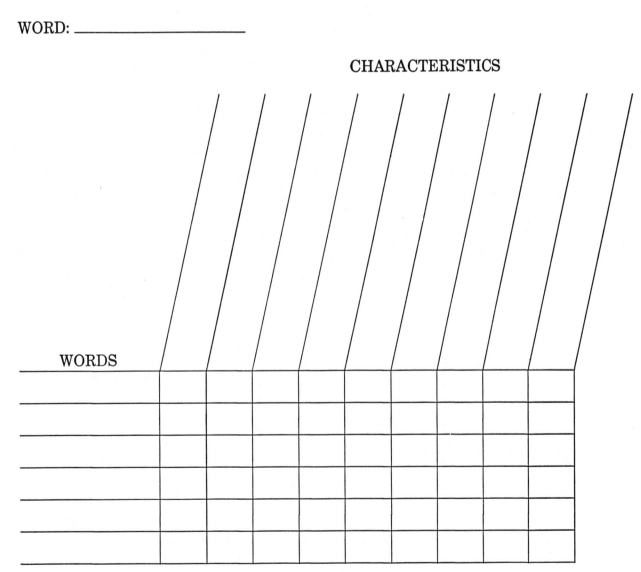

CHARACTERISTICS

WORDS

unit II

DEVELOPING STUDY SKILLS

Unit II presents activities to help develop study skills. The first concept is following oral and written directions. Through the activities, the student is required to give as well as receive directions to be followed. Having students formulate directions helps make them aware of the importance of clarity, sequence, brevity and precise vocabulary. These activities provide a range of experiences in which students may practice following various types of directions.

Students also benefit from deliberate effort on the part of the teacher to give good directions. Before giving a set of oral directions, you should ensure that students are attentive and prepared to receive them. The tendency to repeat oral directions for students does not encourage the development of good listening skills.

The next concept deals with taking notes. As students reach the upper grades, they are increasingly called upon to take notes, and often find themselves writing frantically and missing a great deal of information. The activities provided in this section help a student become more discriminating in both the quantity and quality of information recorded. Through these activities, students should begin to recognize organizational patterns and schemes in materials presented.

The next part of the unit provides activities that help students prepare for a test. The first activity encourages students to anticipate probable topics and questions for a test. This technique helps to direct the students' attention to important concepts and information, thus serving as an effective review. The other activity asks the students to locate the sources of information for test questions. The following hints are often helpful for students taking tests:

1. When studying for a test, spend most of your time on things about which you are most unsure. Don't waste time on things you know.

2. Try to view a test as a measure of learning and relax. A test score in itself should not be the primary concern. Rather, the test should be viewed as an indicator of both accomplishment and areas needing further study.

3. First, read all directions carefully.

4. Look over the entire test before beginning. Getting an overview will allow you to establish a time frame for the test's completion.

5. If a test is divided into sections, each worth a different point value, divide the time accordingly, spending the most effort/time on the most valuable sections.

6. Slow down your rate of reading during a test.

7. Do those questions of which you are sure. Then go back to the others. Don't spend too much time on those items you don't know.

8. Watch for words like "always," "never," "all," and "none." These words suggest situations that include or exclude most responses. Read test items containing these words to evaluate the response.

9. Don't change an answer unless you are really sure about it. Your first response is more often correct.

The last part of Unit II gives two activities to help students organize their time in doing their homework. An analysis of their own use of time and a method of organizing time and assignments are intended to help students efficiently complete their homework.

These study skills activities are designed to reinforce specific skills. Extension activities are also suggested as further reinforcement of these skills.

SKILL: A. Following Directions

OBJECTIVE:
Students will complete a variety of activities to follow written and oral directions and to formulate written and oral directions.

STRATEGIES:
1. Make students aware of the vocabulary used in directions. Signal words (first, next, following, after, and any other time or sequence words) are key to successfully completing a task. For written directions, have students first read the directions and then underline these signal words. Direct them to numerically sequence each step. For oral directions, instruct students to listen for the signal words and then record them.

2. Point out the use of verb commands in direction statements. Most often, these verb commands begin the statements. Point out that this helps simplify and clarify directions.

3. When students formulate directions, strategies 1 and 2 can be used to check the effectiveness of the directions statements.

4. In following or formulating directions, emphasis should be placed on materials. Both the identification of materials and when they are needed should be considered.

5. The audience for which directions are formulated must be taken into account when determining the level of vocabulary and complexity of sentence structure.

6. As students practice following and formulating directions, encourage them to evaluate themselves in an effort to improve their performance. Discuss the problems encountered and have students suggest methods for improvement.

7. In regular classroom teaching, make an effort to give oral directions only once. However, before giving directions, be certain to have the attention of the group.

SPECIAL DIRECTIONS:
"The Helicopter": Once the students have the necessary materials, read the following set of directions:
1. Cut along all solid lines.
2. Fold A toward you.
3. Fold B away from you.
4. Fold C in toward you.
5. Fold D over C.
6. Fold up at E.
7. Hold your arm up and release the helicopter.

TEACHING HINTS:
All of the activities for following and formulating directions may be done in small groups. The more complex activities may be best suited to total class instruction.

ANSWERS:
IIA-2 Having a Birthday Party
Answers may vary and still be correct.
IIA-7 Making Scrambled Eggs
Answers may vary and still be correct. Discuss with students the effects that different sequences have on the completed task. For example, getting out a frying pan may occur in several locations within the sequence. However, breaking the eggs must come before beating the eggs.

II. DEVELOPING STUDY SKILLS   *A. Following Directions*

PAPER AIRPLANE

OBJECTIVE: Completing a task by following written directions
MATERIALS: For this activity, you will need the airplane pattern, and scissors.
PROCEDURE:

1.   Fold the airplane pattern in half as shown.

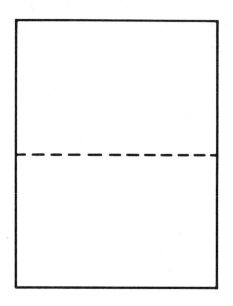

2.   Open the fold and make another fold, about ¼″. Continue folding 10 more times until about 4½″ are left.

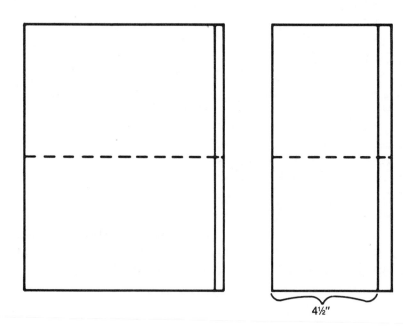

4½″

IIA-1

PAPER AIRPLANE (continued)

3. Fold the pattern in half and cut along the solid lines.

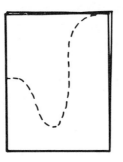

4. Open the plane and fold the wing tips up. Then turn the plane over and fold down the tips of the tail.

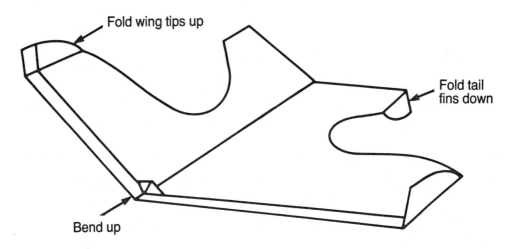

Fold wing tips up

Fold tail fins down

Bend up

5. Fly the finished plane.

    EXTENSION: Go to your library and find a book that gives directions for making other paper planes, origami, wood projects, or simple crafts. To practice the skill of following written directions, try to construct one of these projects.

Name ————————————— Date —————————

AIRPLANE PATTERN

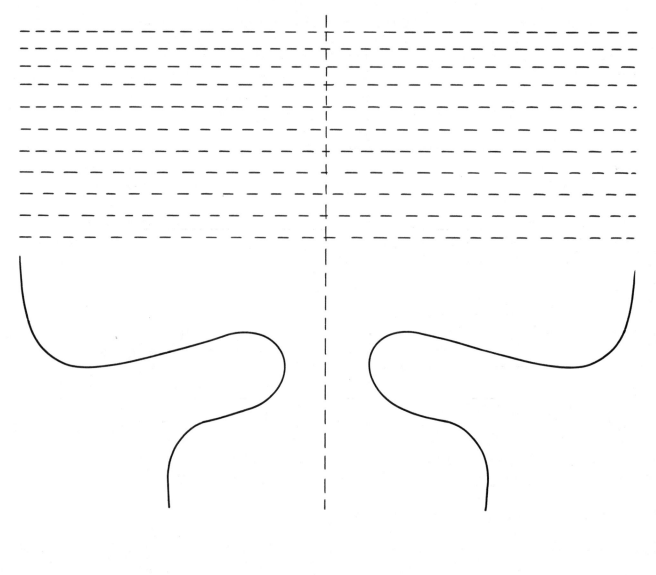

IIA-1 (continued)

II. DEVELOPING STUDY SKILLS   *A. Following Directions*

HAVING A BIRTHDAY PARTY

OBJECTIVE: Sequencing a set of directions in order to complete a task
MATERIALS: For this activity, you will need a pencil.
PROCEDURE: (1) Read all the steps below. (2) Determine a logical order in which to complete the steps. (3) Number the steps appropriately.

_____ Buy decorations
_____ Send invitations
_____ Blow out candles on the cake
_____ Plan activities
_____ Blow up balloons
_____ Discuss party with parents
_____ Open presents
_____ Buy the cake
_____ Decide on the guest list
_____ Set up for the party
_____ Greet guests
_____ Clean up
_____ Have fun

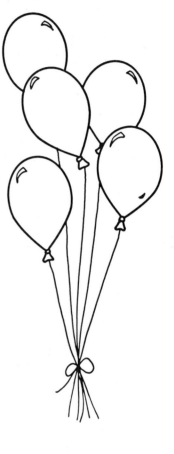

II. DEVELOPING STUDY SKILLS   *A. Following Directions*

THE HELICOPTER

OBJECTIVE: Following oral directions to make a paper "helicopter"
MATERIALS: For this activity, you will need scissors and the pattern below.
PROCEDURE: Follow the directions given to you by your teacher.

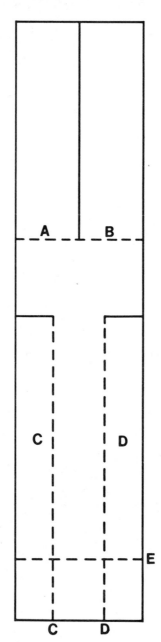

IIA-3

HOW TO DO IT

OBJECTIVE: Writing and following directions for an activity

MATERIALS: For this activity, you will need paper, pencil, and additional materials as needed.

PROCEDURE:

1. Choose an activity for which you will write a set of directions. Possible choices include drawing something, making a simple craft, tying a shoelace, playing a game, or working on a hobby.

2. Make a list of any needed materials. Be sure to choose an activity that requires only available materials.

3. Make a list of the steps as necessary to complete the activity. As you do this, try to visualize all of the things that must be done before the activity is completed.

4. Put the steps into the correct order.

5. Add any hints or additional information to make each step clear and easy to follow.

6. Exchange your set of directions with a classmate and try to follow each other's directions.

7. Were you successful in completing the other person's activity?

   _____ If not, why not? _____

   _____

   _____

8. How could the directions have been better? _____

   _____

   _____

   _____

   _____

   _____

   _____

DIRECTIONS FOR ORIENTEERING

OBJECTIVE: Writing a set of directions for another person to follow

MATERIALS: For this activity, you will need a compass, a meter stick or yardstick, paper, and a pencil.

PROCEDURE:

1. Choose a starting point within your classroom or outside your school. This starting point should be a landmark such as a door, bench, flag pole, etc. On paper, represent this point as Point A.

2. Set the compass to one of these four directions: north, south, east, or west.

3. Choose a direction to follow and use the measuring stick to measure the distance to another point that you choose. This spot should be marked by a tree, rock, chair, bookcase, or other object. Call this Point B. Be sure to record the direction and distance between Point A and Point B.

4. From Point B, choose a new direction. Using the measuring stick, measure the distance to another point. Call this Point C. Record the direction and distance between Point B and Point C.

5. Follow the same procedure to map points D and E. Record the direction and distance for each. Be sure that Point E is a specific landmark as was Point A.

6. Give these directions for a classmate to follow.

7. Check with your classmate to determine whether your directions were clear and accurate. Did your classmate locate Point E correctly? If not, why not? What part of the directions could have been improved?

EXTENSION: Create new sets of orienteering directions. You might select a different geographical setting for this activity.

© 1990 by The Center for Applied Research in Education

PEANUT BUTTER/BANANA EGGNOG

OBJECTIVE: Following directions in a recipe

MATERIALS: For this activity, you will need 1 small ripe banana, 1 egg, 1 cup of cold milk, ½ teaspoon of vanilla, ¼ cup of creamy peanut butter, 1-quart bowl, a whisk or rotary beater, and two glasses.

PROCEDURE:

1.   Do this activity with a classmate. The recipe makes two servings.
2.   Peel the banana and break it into small pieces.
3.   Place the banana, egg, and peanut butter into the bowl. Beat with a wisk or rotary beater until smooth.
4.   Slowly beat in the milk and vanilla.
5.   Pour into two glasses.
6.   Drink it.

EXTENSION: Use a cookbook to practice following recipe directions at home.

II. DEVELOPING STUDY SKILLS   *A. Following Directions*

MAKING SCRAMBLED EGGS

OBJECTIVE: Sequencing a set of directions in order to complete a task

MATERIALS: For this activity, you will need a pencil.

PROCEDURE: (1) Read all the steps below. (2) Determine a logical order in which to complete the steps. (3) Number the steps appropriately.

_____ Break two eggs into a bowl.

_____ Use a spatula to mix the eggs in the frying pan.

_____ Get out a frying pan.

_____ Place the scrambled eggs on a plate.

_____ Beat the two eggs and water.

_____ Take two eggs from the refrigerator.

_____ Remove the scrambled eggs from the frying pan.

_____ Dig in and enjoy.

_____ Melt one tablespoon of butter in the frying pan.

_____ Add two tablespoons of water to the eggs in the bowl.

_____ Pour the beaten eggs into the melted butter in the frying pan.

EXTENSION: For a task with which you are familiar, write a list of directions in random order. Exchange your list with a classmate for proper sequencing.

DO JUST WHAT I SAY

OBJECTIVE: Following and giving oral directions

MATERIALS: For this activity, you will need this directions sheet for Partner A, blank paper for Partner B, a pencil for Partner B, and a ruler for each partner.

PROCEDURE:

1.   Do this activity with a classmate.

2.   Partner A needs this directions sheet and Partner B needs a blank sheet of paper and a pencil.

3.   Sit back to back with your partner.

4.   Partner A must give oral directions to Partner B in order to have Partner B reproduce the figure shown below on the blank paper.

5.   At the conclusion of the activity, Partners A and B should evaluate their abilities in giving and following oral directions and then make suggestions for improvement.

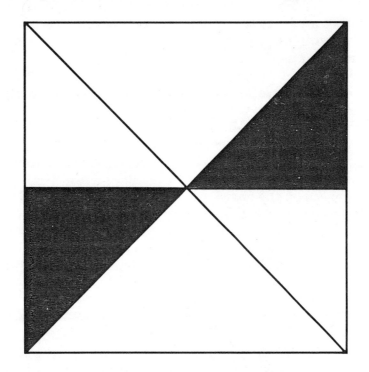

EXTENSION: Partner B should draw an original figure. Then repeat this activity with Partner B giving oral directions so Partner A can try to duplicate the figure.

SKILL: B. Listening

OBJECTIVE:
Students will listen to oral presentations in order to record and recall information.

STRATEGIES:
1. Make students aware of focusing techniques to help improve their listening skills, such as attending to the speaker and tuning out distractions.
2. Give students a clearly stated purpose for listening.

SPECIAL DIRECTIONS:

"Dictation"

Explain to the students that you are going to read a list of sentences, one sentence at a time. You will read each sentence only one time; you will not repeat any direction. Instruct students to listen to the entire sentence before writing it. Their purpose in listening during this activity is to be able to copy down each word dictated in the order as it is spoken.

Dictate the following:

I left the suitcase over there by the gate. (*Pause to allow students to write it.*)

Their suitcases were not anywhere to be found. (*Pause*)

They're friends of mine from Miami, Florida. (*Pause*)

The airline is known for their service. (*Pause*)

Their tickets were lost over there by the entrance, and they're not very happy about it. (*Pause*)

Record the sentences on the board or overhead transparency. Have students check their papers. Notice that in this activity, a spelling homonym (their, there, they're) is reviewed. Both listening and spelling skills are being developed.

An extension of "Dictation" is to design sentences containing content information. For example, you may dictate sentences dealing with geometry, constellations, vocabulary, etc.

"Recall the Facts"

Explain to the class that you are going to read a short summary of an incident. Instruct students to listen carefully as if they were private detectives as they will be asked to recall information presented in the article. Read aloud the following article once at a reasonable pace:

It was about 7:15 a.m. when I was traveling north on Main Street. Since I had an early appointment with a customer, I decided I had better get to work early to organize my desk.

As I was nearing the intersection of Main Street and Lane Avenue, I heard a screeching sound from behind. Upon looking in my rear view mirror, I saw the horrified look on the young driver's face in the front seat. Before I knew it, my three-year-old car was jolted forward. I was then hit by a pick-up truck that was coming from the east.

Chris Matthews, the driver of the car that hit me in the rear, Gerry Anderson, the driver of the pick-up, and I exchanged licenses and insurance information.

During the exchange of licenses, Officer Thomas arrived on the scene in patrol car number 47.

By the time I arrived at work, I had missed my 8:30 a.m. appointment.
(*End of reading*)

Next, distribute the handout and have students answer the questions from memory.

You can do this same activity using articles from newspapers, magazines, textbooks, etc.

"Draw Me"

Once students have the necessary materials, read the following set of directions:

1. Draw a straight line from D to A.
2. Draw a straight line from D to C.
3. Extend the line from B downward ½ inch.
4. Draw a line parallel to ABC so that it touches the bottom of the line you just drew. Make the new line one inch longer on each end than line ABC.
5. Label one end of this new line E and the other end F.
6. Draw another line one inch below and parallel to line EF. Make this line the same length as line AC.
7. Connect E to the closer end of the last line you drew and connect F to the other end.

TEACHING HINTS:

You may want to consider the seating arrangement in your classroom when teaching listening skills. All students should be able to make eye contact with the speaker, hear the speaker clearly, and have minimal distractions.

ANSWERS:

IIB-2 Recall the Facts

1. three
2. had an early appointment
3. Main Street and Lane Avenue
4. Gerry Anderson
5. 47
6. licenses and insurance information
7. west
8. after 8:30 a.m.
9. narrator is not identified

II. DEVELOPING STUDY SKILLS   *B. Listening*

DICTATION

OBJECTIVE: Recording information on paper once it has been stated verbally

MATERIALS: For this activity, you will need paper and a pencil.

PROCEDURE:

1.   Your teacher will read a list of sentences, one sentence at a time. The sentences will not be read a second time.

2.   You will listen to each sentence and then write it exactly as you recall it. Your goal is to write each word dictated and in the exact order it was read.

SENTENCES:

1. _____

_____

_____

2. _____

_____

_____

3. _____

_____

_____

4. _____

_____

_____

5. _____

_____

_____

Name _____ Date _____

II. DEVELOPING STUDY SKILLS   *B. Listening*

RECALL THE FACTS

OBJECTIVE: Listening to recall information
MATERIALS: For this activity, you will need a pencil.
PROCEDURE: (1) Listen as your teacher reads a short passage. (2) Then answer as many of the questions below as you can. Be as accurate as possible. (3) Listen as your teacher rereads the passage and correct your answers as you listen.

1. How many vehicles were involved in the accident? _____

2. For what reason was the person telling the story going to work earlier than usual?
    _____

3. At the intersection of which two roads did the accident occur? _____
    _____

4. What was the name of the driver of the pick-up truck? _____
    _____

5. What was the number of the patrol car that came to the scene of the accident? _____
    _____

6. What two items did the drivers exchange at the scene? _____
    _____

7. In what direction was the pick-up truck going when it struck the car? _____
    _____

8. What time did the teller of the story arrive at work? _____

9. What was the name of the person telling the story? _____
    _____

II. DEVELOPING STUDY SKILLS   *B. Listening*

GET THE FACTS

OBJECTIVE: Listening for key information in a news article

MATERIALS: For this activity, you will need a news article and a pencil.

PROCEDURE: (1) Bring an interesting news article to class. (2) Read your article aloud to a classmate. (3) Have your classmate answer the following questions. (4) Discuss and verify the answers with the news article.

1. Who or what is the article about?

   _____

   _____

2. What happened?

   _____

   _____

3. Where did it happen?

   _____

   _____

4. When?

   _____

   _____

5. Why did it happen?

   _____

   _____

6. How did it happen?

   _____

   _____

II. DEVELOPING STUDY SKILLS   *B. Listening*

DRAW ME

OBJECTIVE: Drawing a figure from oral directions

MATERIALS: For this activity, you will need a pencil, a ruler, and the pattern below.

PROCEDURE: Listen carefully and then follow each direction given to you by your teacher.

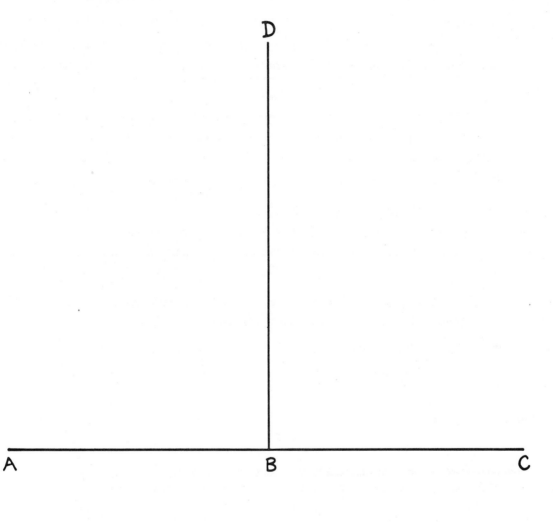

SKILL: C. Taking Notes

OBJECTIVE:
Students will use outlining, identification of vocabulary terms and their relationships, highlighting information, and clustering as techniques for taking notes.

STRATEGIES:
1. Point out to students that taking notes is a short cut by which they select the more important information to be remembered. Time is more efficiently used through proper identification and recording of the key points in a passage.

2. Point out the use of titles, subtitles, bold-faced terms, italicized type, and other context clues that indicate terms and ideas of importance. These clues also indicate relationships among terms and ideas.

3. Make students aware of signal words that are used to show relationships among ideas. These words are used to show chronological order, spatial relations, comparison/contrast, cause/effect, etc.

4. Once students have taken notes, have them use their notes as a way of learning the material. The taking of notes and the subsequent use of these notes in reviewing help students learn concepts and improve retention. Make reviewing notes a regular part of the class routine. Students' notes can be used to answer study questions, anticipate test questions, construct outlines, and write summaries.

SPECIAL DIRECTIONS:

"Listening for Information"
   Read the following passage about fish. Then have students fill in the accompanying outline.

FISH
   What animal has no eyelids and sleeps with its eyes open? Some kinds are less than one half inch long and others are over sixty feet long. They come in colors such as red, blue, yellow, purple, and green, and they may be spotted or striped. Some have lumps, some have spines, some look like rocks, some are flat, and some inflate like balloons. Were you able to guess the animal is a fish? Although you may notice many differences, there are three characteristics common to all fish. First, all fish have a backbone. For this reason fish are called vertebrates. Second, fish breathe through organs called gills. Third, fish cannot control their own body temperature. Because of this, they are called cold-blooded animals. Cold-blooded means that the fish's body temperature will change with the temperature of the environment.
   Although fish have these three characteristics in common, the fish of the world can be divided into two main categories. Some fish are jawless, while others have a jaw. The hagfish and the lamprey are the only two fish known to belong to the jawless group. Most of the fish we know have jaws. Trout, catfish, and sharks are some of the fish with jaws.

If you were to examine the body of a fish, you could divide the body into three main sections. The first part would be the head. The head contains the mouth, eyes, nostrils, gills, and scales. The second part of the fish is the trunk. The trunk has the dorsal fins, the pelvic fins, and the pectoral fins. Finally, there is the tail section. The tail consists of fins which help the fish to move.

"Highlighting"

For this activity, use a duplicated copy of a passage so that students can highlight without marking the pages of a book.

ANSWERS:

IIC-1 Listening for Information

I. Characteristics of fish
   A. Have a backbone
   B. Breathe through gills
   C. Cannot control their temperature

II. Categories of fish
   A. Jawless fish
      1. hagfish
      2. lamprey
   B. Fish with jaws
      1. and 2. Examples: trout, catfish, or sharks

III. Physical features of fish
   A. Head
      1. mouth
      2. eyes
      3. nostrils
      4. gills
      5. scales
   B. Trunk
      1. dorsal fins
      2. pelvic fins
      3. pectoral fins
   C. Tail

IIC-6 Picture It

2. Key facts: Vultures use sight, not smell, to locate prey; they circle above prey. When a vulture spots prey, it drops down to investigate. This signals other vultures to do the same.

4. Students' illustrations should communicate the information presented in number 2.

II. DEVELOPING STUDY SKILLS   *C. Taking Notes*

LISTENING FOR INFORMATION

OBJECTIVE: Completing an outline while listening to an oral presentation

MATERIALS: For this activity, you will need a pencil and the outline handout.

PROCEDURE:

1.   Your teacher is going to read a passage. As it is being read, listen for the main ideas presented and the supporting details for each main idea.

2.   Your teacher will give you a partially completed outline. As you listen to your teacher read the passage, complete the outline.

Name _____ Date _____

OUTLINE HANDOUT
Fish

I. Characteristics of fish

   A. _____

   B. _____

   C. _____

II. Categories of fish
   A. Jawless fish

      1. Example: _____

      2. Example: _____

   B. Fish with jaws:

      1. Example: _____

      2. Example: _____

III. Physical features of fish
   A. Head

      1. _____

      2. _____

      3. _____

      4. _____

      5. _____

   B. Trunk

      1. _____

      2. _____

      3. _____

   C. Tail

II. DEVELOPING STUDY SKILLS   *C. Taking Notes*

LISTENING FOR THE MAIN POINTS

OBJECTIVE: Taking notes from an audio-visual presentation

MATERIALS: For this activity, you will need paper, a pencil, and the handout.

PROCEDURE:

1. Your teacher will show you an audio-visual presentation. When viewing such a presentation, you will be listening for information. While you are viewing, you are going to write some notes to help you remember what you saw and heard. Here are some tips to remember when taking notes:

   • Write down only important things. Do not try to write down everything.

   • Keep things brief.

   • Write in short phrases; complete sentences are not needed in your notes.

   • Listen for key vocabulary words and definitions.

   • Pay special attention to concluding and summarizing statements.

2. Use the handout to fill in information you see and hear during the presentation.

3. Once you have finished, discuss the information you recorded with your class.

EXTENSION: Using the information you have recorded, reorganize the information into an outline. Based upon the outline, write a summary of the presentation.

Name _____ Date _____

AUDIO-VISUAL PRESENTATION NOTE-TAKING HANDOUT

Title: _____

MAIN IDEA	SUPPORTING DETAILS AND EXAMPLES	KEY TERMS AND DEFINITIONS

Summarizing Statements:

1. _____

2. _____

Use the back of this sheet if you need more space to write.

II. DEVELOPING STUDY SKILLS   *C. Taking Notes*

OUTLINING

OBJECTIVE: Developing an outline using the headings, subheadings, and main ideas from a section of a textbook.

MATERIALS: For this activity, you will need a pencil, paper, and a textbook lesson.

PROCEDURE:

1. Open your textbook to the reading selection your teacher has assigned you. Skim the pages to get an idea of what the reading passage is about. This idea is the subject or topic of the reading.

2. Next, pay attention to the use of headings and subheadings. These are important clues to the main points that the author is making about the subject. Some headings will appear in larger or darker type than others. These are headings, whereas ideas in smaller or lighter type are subheadings.

3. Now, look under one of the subheadings. There will be a series of paragraphs that explain or discuss the subheading. Each paragraph usually will give information about a separate idea within the subheading.

4. You can see, then, that the author has a way of organizing information for the reader. You can use this arrangement of information to outline the main points of the reading:

   a. The subject of the reading can become the title of your outline.

   b. The headings can become the Roman numerals of your outline.

   c. The subheadings can become the supporting details of your Roman numerals.

   d. The main ideas of the paragraphs can become the supporting details of your subheadings.

This would result in an outline looking something like this:

Title

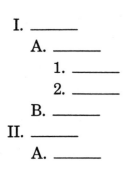

I. _____
   A. _____
      1. _____
      2. _____
   B. _____
II. _____
   A. _____

OUTLINING (continued)

5. Using this method, develop an outline for the reading passage assigned to you by your teacher. This outline can then be used as a study tool when reviewing for quizzes and tests.

6. When you are done, compare your outline with those of your classmates. Discuss the differences.

EXTENSION: Select another section of your textbook and outline it as described in the procedure.

HIGHLIGHTING

OBJECTIVE: Highlighting main ideas and supporting details

MATERIALS: For this activity, you will need a copy of a reading selection with headings and subheadings, and a highlighter marker.

PROCEDURE:

1. In addition to the outlining strategy for taking notes, another method that uses the same principles is called highlighting. Instead of recording the main ideas and supporting details on paper, you highlight them on the written page. Before using this strategy, be sure that you are not highlighting a text that does not belong to you.

2. In the selected reading passage, highlight the headings and subheadings in the passage.

3. In each paragraph under these headings and subheadings, highlight the main idea sentence for each paragraph.

4. Highlight any important terms and definitions.

EXTENSION: Using the information that you have highlighted, write a summary of the reading passage.

Name _____ Date _____

KEY WORDS

OBJECTIVE: Recording vocabulary terms and their definitions from a selected reading

MATERIALS: For this activity, you will need a pencil and a dictionary or glossary from a textbook.

PROCEDURE:

1. When reading a passage that contains words and ideas that are new to you, it is important to focus your attention on these words. In this activity, you will do just that.

2. As you read the selection, record the new words and phrases on the chart below. If the selection provides the definition, write it in the space under "Meaning." If not, use the glossary of your text or a dictionary.

3. At the conclusion of your reading, discuss your words and definitions with the class. Throughout the discussion, you can add information and refine the definitions you have.

WORDS/PHRASES	MEANING

EXTENSION: Write a summary of the reading selection by using the key words and phrases within your summary.

Name _____ Date _____

PICTURE IT

OBJECTIVE: Designing and constructing a visual display to include key concepts and terminology from a reading

MATERIALS: For this activity, you will need colored pencils, drawing paper, and the "Vultures" reading handout.

PROCEDURE:

1. Read the "Vultures" handout.

2. In this note-taking strategy, you will design a picture or series of pictures that will explain the main ideas presented in the reading. The goal of this activity is not the artwork but a better understanding of the material. Before you begin drawing, think about what the handout said. What is the handout about and what is the author saying about the topic?

3. Once you have done this, ask yourself what picture or pictures you could sketch to help you remember what you have read.

4. Sketch the illustration(s) and be prepared to explain your picture(s) to the class.

© 1990 by The Center for Applied Research in Education

VULTURES

As dusk settles on the desert, the dark form of the dead coyote becomes the center of great activity. The gentle winds blow tumbleweed across the dry sand. High above, a lonely vulture circles the sky in search of food. Since most birds have no sense of smell, the vulture depends on its keen eyesight to find food. As the vulture searches, it flies in large circles scanning the ground below. When it sees a dead animal, the vulture drops to investigate. This dropping motion is a signal to nearby circling vultures, who then also come to investigate. The movement of these vultures signals others even farther away. Within a short time, many vultures are feeding on the dead coyote.

Did You Know?
Vultures have no feathers on their heads. The head feathers would become matted with blood and decaying material from feeding on dead animals. Having no head feathers helps the vulture stay clean.

SKILL: D. Studying and Taking Tests

OBJECTIVE:
Students will complete a variety of activities to increase their awareness about the kinds of information included on tests, help them anticipate these questions, and learn some strategies in preparing for a test.

STRATEGIES:

1.   Help students see that there is a logical way to study for a test. Test items come from the readings. Students can be shown how to anticipate a test question.

2.   Take time to show students how you construct a test. For a test you have given, show them from where you took your questions.

3.   Prior to a test, have a discussion with students in which they anticipate possible test items.

Name _____ Date _____

STUDY GUIDE

OBJECTIVE: Reviewing a unit of study in preparation for a test

MATERIALS: For this activity, you will need a pencil, the "Study Guide" handout, and books, notes, quizzes, assignments, and any other materials from a completed unit of study.

PROCEDURE:

1. Look through the books, notes, quizzes, assignments, and any other materials used during the unit of study.

2. Fill in the important information in each of the categories on the "Study Guide" handout.

3. Use the information on the "Study Guide" handout to make up some questions you think might be asked on the test.

EXTENSION: After the test, compare the "Study Guide" with the test. Determine the types of questions asked and the kinds of information covered. How well did you anticipate the questions and kinds of information covered on your test? How might you improve your study guide on the next test?

Topic: _____

Important Vocabulary and Definitions:

1. _____

2. _____

3. _____

4. _____

5. _____

Name _____ Date _____

Main Idea #1: _____
Details and Examples

A. _____

B. _____

C. _____

Main Idea #2: _____
Details and Examples

A. _____

B. _____

C. _____

Main Idea #3: _____
Details and Examples

A. _____

B. _____

C. _____

Relationships Within Topic:

Sequence _____

_____

Cause and Effect _____

_____

Comparison and Contrast _____

_____

Fact and Opinion _____

_____

Conclusions:

1. _____

2. _____

3. _____

IID-1 (continued)

Name _____ Date _____

A STUDY GUIDE STRATEGY

OBJECTIVE: Reading for studying

MATERIALS: For this activity, you will need a pencil, textbook pages or notebook pages from which you can study, and the "Study Guide Chart."

PROCEDURE:

1. For this activity, you should have in front of you the textbook pages or notebook pages relating to your current area of study. If you use notebook pages, number them in order before beginning this activity.

2. Starting with the first page, enter the page number in the first column. Then ask a question that you could answer from the reading material on this page. This should also be a question that you anticipate could be on a quiz or test. Record this question in column two. Then record your answer to the question in column three. Continue asking questions about this page until you exhaust the possibilities. Then go on to the next page. Here is a sample study guide entry:

PAGE NUMBER	QUESTION	ANSWER
1	Who were the two opponents in the U.S. Civil War?	the North and the South

3. When you have completed your study guide questions, ask a partner the questions you have written down. Also have your partner ask you his or her questions. This will help both you and your partner to learn this material.

STUDY GUIDE CHART

PAGE NUMBER	QUESTION	ANSWER

IID-2 (continued)

© 1990 by The Center for Applied Research in Education

II. DEVELOPING STUDY SKILLS   *D. Studying and Taking Tests*

TEST ANALYSIS

OBJECTIVE: Analyzing a test to improve effectiveness in studying

MATERIALS: For this activity, you will need a pencil, a textbook, and paper.

PROCEDURE:

1. After completing a chapter in your textbook, locate the end-of-the-chapter test.

2. Take the test and score it. Correct any incorrect answers.

3. Circle the number of the questions on your test paper that ask about vocabulary from the chapter. How many are there? _____

4. Read the chapter summary if one is present. Put an X over the numbers of the questions that can be answered with information found in the summary. How many are there? _____

5. Read the headings and subheadings in the chapter. How many questions can be answered using these? _____

6. Read the first paragraph after each subheading of the chapter. Draw a star in front of the numbers of the questions that can be answered with information found in the first paragraphs. How many are there? _____

7. Read the captions for the pictures in the chapter. How many questions can be answered with information found in the captions? _____

8. Look at any graphs, charts, diagrams, or other drawings in the chapter. How many questions can be answered using these? _____

9. Check any special features that may appear in the chapter, such as news articles, special interest articles, or investigations. Are these features used to form questions? _____ If so, how many? _____

10. Determine where the answers may be found for any test questions not already located.

11. How should you study for another test in this textbook? _____

_____

_____

_____

_____

SKILL: E. Doing Homework

OBJECTIVE:
Students will try strategies for organizing their time and completing homework assignments.

STRATEGIES:
1. As greater homework demands are placed on the student in the middle grades, it is important to help show the student how to schedule time at home.
2. Students can benefit from assistance in the recording of the assignment in the classroom, maintaining an organized notebook, and monitoring their use of time.
3. Have students keep their assignment sheets in a notebook. This way, they can refer back to previous assignments.

Name _____ Date _____

WHERE DOES THE TIME GO?

OBJECTIVE: Maintaining a log of homework assignment completion and time spent

MATERIALS: For this activity, you will need a pencil and the "Homework Log Sheet."

PROCEDURE:

1. In this strategy, you will take time to maintain a homework log for a specified period of time. This log will have you keep track of the time you spend at home after school: homework time, watching television, eating, playing with friends, talking on the phone, etc.

2. Each day, enter the day's date. Then keep track of what you do from the time you get home from school until you go to bed. A sample log for a day is shown below:

    Monday

    3:30-4   math homework page 8, problems 3-24

    4-5:30   played basketball with some friends

    6-7:00   ate dinner

    7-8:00   English homework (rough draft of story)

    8-9:00   watched television

    9-10:00   read a mystery, chapters 1 and 2

    10:00   lights out, went to bed

3. On the final day of the log, bring it to school and compare your results with those of your classmates. Then consider whether your use of time was efficient.

HOMEWORK LOG SHEET

Student: _____   From___/___/___ to ___/___/___

	M	T	W	TH	F
3:30–4					
4–4:30					
4:30–5					
5–5:30					
5:30–6					
6–6:30					
6:30–7					
7–7:30					
7:30–8					
8–8:30					
8:30–9					
9–9:30					
9:30–10					
10–10:30					
10:30–11					

IIE-1 (continued)

Name _____ Date _____

ASSIGNMENT SHEET

OBJECTIVE: Completing an assignment sheet to organize and keep track of homework assignments

MATERIALS: For this activity, you will need a pencil and the "Assignment Sheet" handout.

PROCEDURE: Use this assignment sheet to record each homework assignment you get during the week. Write down the subject, the assignment, the due date, and check when it is completed. Record any long-range assignments and their due dates in the space provided.

ASSIGNMENT SHEET

Assignments for ____/____/____

SUBJECT	ASSIGNMENT	DUE DATE	COMPLETED

Long-Term Assignments:

SUBJECT	ASSIGNMENT	DUE DATE	COMPLETED

unit III
LOCATING INFORMATION SKILLS

Unit III presents activities to help develop the student's ability to locate information using a variety of resources. An increasingly information-based world demands that people be able to use available resources.

The first skill to be developed is using a textbook. The textbook for students is often the most immediate and often-used source of information. However, for many students the textbook is an overwhelming obstacle to be faced each time they have an assignment. Through a variety of activities, students are taught the organizational structure of the textbook. Once students are taught this organizational scheme, they are able to use the text more efficiently.

From using the textbook, we move to a larger source of information: the library. The library is a vast source of information, and, with our advances today in various forms of data collection, it will continue to grow more complex. Students need to be made aware of the library systems that enable them to find information. The activities in this part of the unit help students to see the library as a more manageable source of information.

Beyond the library, students are shown the importance of being able to read to survive the everyday demands of living in our society. From filling out forms to reading product labels on food, students are shown how to locate information in the world around them. Many of the sources of information we use everyday are designed around an organizational scheme. When this scheme is learned, students are more comfortable in using these everyday sources. Activities in this section focus on forms, telephone books, newspapers, signs, maps, labels, and catalogs.

These skills are designed to help students locate information using the sources of information that they meet both in school and out of school. All of these sources have an organizational scheme that when recognized allows students to use them more efficiently.

SKILL: A. Using a Textbook

OBJECTIVE:

Students will complete a variety of activities to help them develop their skill in using the main parts of the textbook.

STRATEGIES:

1. Help students to see that a textbook has a variety of parts, with each part serving a particular function. Have students open their texts and identify the following parts and their functions:

    Title page

    Table of contents

    Unit/chapter/lesson organizers (introductory section, main text, summary activities)

    Glossary

    Index

2. Alert students to an author's use of text style and color as clues to the organization of information. Bold type may be used for titles, subtitles, and vocabulary. Teachers may want to point out the use of color/logos to indicate special features.

3. Have students make predictions as to the content of a particular chapter or reading based upon the chapter title or headings and subheadings. After introducing students to prediction, you may want to employ this strategy on a regular basis.

4. Once students have received instruction in the various parts of the textbook, have students use these parts in their lessons. Instead of telling them to turn to a specific page, tell them the chapter title and have them use the table of contents to find the page it begins on.

TEACHING HINTS:

If students lack background, these activities are most effective when done as teaching through discussion.

For the activity "How Are Headings and Subheadings Organized?" it is effective to use the overhead projector. Make a transparency of the headings and subheadings and complete this activity with the class. Have the students follow along at their desks with their own set of strips.

ANSWERS:

IIIA-1 How Can a Table of Contents Help?

1. Student responses will vary. Have students provide a rationale for their responses.

2. four

3. four
4. Unit titles are in all capital letters while chapter titles are in lower case.
5. Chapter titles are indented under their unit title.
6. 14
7. 1; 16
8. 62; 70
9. 105
10. before; Roman numerals appear before the Arabic numerals
11. You can't tell from the information presented.

IIIA-2 What's in the Chapter?
Student responses will vary. Have students give their rationale for their responses.

IIIA-3 How Can an Index Help?
1. two; they are out to the left and in all capital letters
2. activities of
3. A hyphen includes all pages between the two indicated, while a comma indicates that only the pages listed will contain the information.
4. yes; 245-248
5. no; 236, 252
6. Eucalyptus; there is a See Also reference
7. Kangaroos
8. alphabetically

IIIA-4 What's in the Index?
Student responses will vary. Have students give their rationale for their responses.

IIIA-5 How Can a Glossary Help?
1. alphabetically
2. frond and Fungi
3. pronunciation of the word
4. page 193
5. A food web involves a number of food chains.
6. a. boldface type
   b. all capital letters indicate syllable with stress, lower case letters indicate syllable without stress
   c. same lettering as glossary word with lighter type
   d. page appears in italics

IIIA-9 How Are Headings and Subheadings Organized?

Overall topic:	The Statue of Liberty
Main headings:	Physical Characteristics
	Geographical Location
	Centennial Celebration
Subheadings:	Student responses will vary. Have them give their rationale for their responses.

HOW CAN A TABLE OF CONTENTS HELP?

OBJECTIVE: Answering questions about a table of contents

MATERIALS: For this activity, you will need a pencil and the "Table of Contents" handout.

PROCEDURE: Study the table of contents in the handout. Take notice of the various pieces of information that it presents about the textbook. After examining the table of contents carefully, answer the following questions.

1. What might the title be for the book in which this table of contents is located?

_____

2. How many units are in this book? _____

3. How many chapters are in unit two? _____

4. How are chapter titles different from unit titles?

_____

5. How does the table of contents show that chapter titles belong to a particular unit?

_____

6. How many chapters are in this book? _____

7. On what page does unit one begin? _____ end? _____

8. On what page does chapter 10 begin? _____ end? _____

9. On what page does the glossary begin? _____

10. Does the introduction of the book appear before page one or after page one? _____

    How can you tell? _____

11. On which page does the index end? _____

© 1990 by The Center for Applied Research in Education

TABLE OF CONTENTS

IIIA-1 (continued)

WHAT'S IN THE CHAPTER?

OBJECTIVE: Anticipating a text's content from a table of contents

MATERIALS: For this activity, you will need a pencil and the "Table of Contents" handout (see activity IIIA-1).

PROCEDURE:

1. Using this table of contents, you are going to write questions that you believe would be answered in the book. For example, it is reasonable to expect that the question "Where was the inventor of the Slinky born?" would be answered in Unit Three, Chapter 10.

2. For each part of the textbook listed below, write one question that you believe would be answered in that section of the text.

Unit One—Chapter One:

_____

Unit One—Chapter Two:

_____

Unit One—Chapter Three:

_____

Unit Two—Chapter Four:

_____

Unit Two—Chapter Five:

_____

Unit Two—Chapter Six:

_____

Unit Two—Chapter Seven:

_____

Unit Three—Chapter Eight:

_____

WHAT'S IN THE CHAPTER? (continued)

Unit Three—Chapter Nine:

_____

Unit Three—Chapter Ten:

_____

Unit Four—Chapter Eleven:

_____

Unit Four—Chapter Twelve:

_____

Unit Four—Chapter Thirteen:

_____

Unit Four—Chapter Fourteen:

_____

EXTENSION: Try this same activity for a table of contents in one of your textbooks. Attempt to answer the questions you proposed using the information in each chapter.

HOW CAN AN INDEX HELP?

OBJECTIVE: Completing a set of questions about a sample index
MATERIALS: For this activity, you will need a pencil and the "Index" handout.
PROCEDURE: Study the handout. Then answer the following questions.

1. How many main topics are listed in this sample part of an index? _____

   How can you tell? _____

   _____

2. Under KOALA BEARS is a series of subtopics. Under which subtopic would you find information about their sleeping patterns?

   _____

3. What is the difference between a hyphen (-) and a comma (,) when looking at page numbers in an index?

   _____

   _____

4. Would you find information about the koala's mating behavior on page 247? _____

   How can you tell? _____

   _____

5. Would you find information on the popularity of the koala bear on page 246? _____

   How can you tell? _____

   _____

6. Under what topic could you look if you wanted to know more about the habitat of the koala bear?

   _____

   How do you know to look under this subtopic? _____

   _____

HOW CAN AN INDEX HELP? (continued)

7. For which animal—the kangaroo or the koala—would you find information on its

    territories? _____

8. How are the topics and subtopics of an index arranged? _____

INDEX

K

Kangaroos
  physical characteristics, 200-213
  territories, 198–199
Koala Bears
  activities of, 235
  breeding habits, 245-248
  foods of, 237, 239-244
  habitat, 248-249
    See also Eucalyptus.
  habits
    eating, 238
    mating, 245-248
  popularity of, 236, 252

WHAT'S IN THE INDEX?

OBJECTIVE: Anticipating questions that could be answered from various subtopics in an index

MATERIALS: For this activity, you will need a pencil and the "Index" handout from activity IIIA-3.

PROCEDURE: For each page number below, find what subtopic will be discussed on that specific page. Then think of a question that would probably be answered on that page. Write your question in the space provided.

Page Number   **Question**

201   _____

_____

235   _____

_____

240   _____

_____

248   _____

_____

252   _____

_____

EXTENSION: Try this same activity for a section of the index in one of your textbooks. Try to answer these questions by using the information on specific text pages listed.

HOW CAN A GLOSSARY HELP?

OBJECTIVE: Answering questions about a glossary
MATERIALS: For this activity, you will need a pencil and the "Glossary" handout.
PROCEDURE: Using the sample glossary, answer the following questions.

1. How are the words arranged?

    _____

2. Between which two words would the word "fruit" appear?

    _____ and _____

3. What information is provided in the parentheses following the word?

    _____

4. On which page would you find more information about the word "flower"?

    _____

5. What is the difference between a food chain and a food web?

    _____

    _____

6. How is the type (lettering form, size, and darkness) different for each of the following?

    a. glossary term: _____

    b. pronunciation: _____

    c. definition: _____

    d. page reference: _____

© 1990 by The Center for Applied Research in Education

SAMPLE GLOSSARY

flower   The reproductive structure of an angiosperm. *p. 193*

food chain   The transfer of energy from one organism to another through food. *p. 329*

food web   An overlapping of food chains in an ecosystem. *p. 330*

fossil (FAHS uhl)   The remains or a trace of an organism that lived in the past. *p. 204*

fossil fuels   Fuels that were formed over millions of years from the remains of once-living things. *p. 420*

frond   The mature leaf of a fern. *p. 181*

Fungi   A major classification group; the kingdom that contains living things that are not green and that do not make their own food. *p. 23*

fungus (FUHN guhs)   An organism that lacks chlorophyll, produces spores, and absorbs food from living or once-living things. *p. 160*

WHAT'S IN A GLOSSARY?

OBJECTIVE: Developing a glossary for a given reading

MATERIALS: For this activity, you will need a reading passage, paper, a pencil, and a dictionary.

PROCEDURE:

1. Read the selected reading passage that has been assigned to you by your teacher.
2. As you read the passage, identify those words that are necessary to the specific topic about which you are reading. These should be words that are related to the topic.
3. Make a list of these words on the lines below.
4. When you are done reading, arrange your list of words alphabetically.
5. Using a dictionary, develop a sample glossary for this specific reading passage. For each word, be sure to include these parts:

   the word

   phonetic spelling for pronunciation

   definition(s)

_____

_____

_____

_____

_____

_____

_____

_____

_____

Name _____ Date _____

HOW IS A TEXTBOOK ORGANIZED?

OBJECTIVE: Analyzing the organizational cues of a lesson in a textbook

MATERIALS: For this activity, you will need a pencil and a lesson in your textbook.

PROCEDURE:

1. Textbooks are designed to help students learn about specific content. In preparing such a book, the authors are careful to arrange the information in such a way as to make it easier for you to grasp. Here are some of the features that an author will use to make text material more understandable:

type size	questions
weight of type (boldface, lightface, etc.)	summaries
style of type (italics, block, etc.)	illustrations
spacing	special features (triangles, dots, asterisks, logos, etc.)
color variations	

2. Examine the text passage you have before you. See how many of these features listed above are used in the passage. Indicate with a "yes" or "no" if the text passage has any of the features.

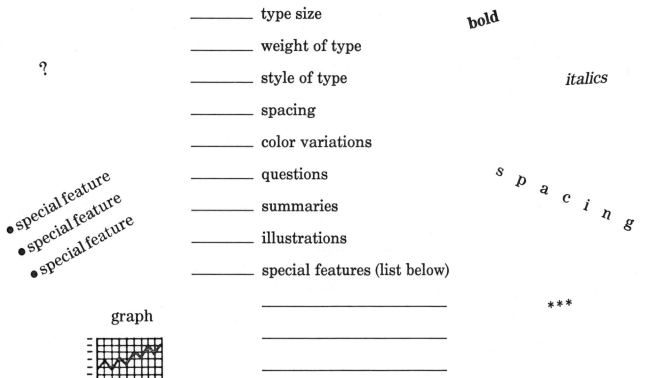

?

_____ type size

bold

_____ weight of type

_____ style of type

italics

_____ spacing

_____ color variations

_____ questions

ˢᵖᵃᶜⁱⁿᵍ

• special feature
 • special feature
  • special feature

_____ summaries

_____ illustrations

_____ special features (list below)

_____

***

graph

_____

_____

WHAT'S IN A LESSON?

OBJECTIVE: Using headings and subheadings to anticipate the content of a text's passage

MATERIALS: For this activity, you will need a lesson in your textbook and a pencil.

PROCEDURE:

1. Examine the lesson in your text for its use of headings and subheadings. Consider the use of the style, size, and weight of the type to determine which are headings and which are subheadings.

2. Once you have done this, copy down the first heading. Under this heading, write two questions that you think will be answered in this section of the text.

3. Next, copy the first subheading under this heading. Under this subheading, write two questions that you think will be answered in this section of the text.

4. Continue this process until you have recorded all of the headings and subheadings with your proposed questions. (Use the back of this sheet and any other additional paper you may need.)

5. Be prepared to share your questions with the class.

EXTENSION: Use the text passage to try and answer your proposed questions.

_____

_____

_____

_____

_____

_____

_____

_____

_____

_____

HOW ARE HEADINGS AND SUBHEADINGS ORGANIZED?

OBJECTIVE: Arranging a group of headings and subheadings into a logical order

MATERIALS: For this activity, you will need the headings/subheadings strips and scissors.

PROCEDURE:

1. Cut out each strip.

2. Examine each strip. Take careful note of various clues that can help you to arrange them into a logical order.

3. First find what you believe are the main headings. Place these in separate columns. Consider which heading should come first, then second, etc.

4. Now find which subheadings belong under each of the main headings. Position them in the correct column. Position them in a logical order.

5. Be prepared to discuss your answers with the class.

THE STATUE OF LIBERTY

PHYSICAL CHARACTERISTICS

New York Harbor

Height

Between George Washington and Verrazano Narrow's Bridges

GEOGRAPHICAL LOCATION

Materials Used to Construct Lady Liberty

CENTENNIAL CELEBRATION

Midway Between New Jersey and New York

Weight

A Hollywood Salute to Lady Liberty

President Reagan Lights Torch

Vietnamese Girl Reads Her Prize-winning Essay

SKILL:　B. Using the Library

OBJECTIVE:
Students will complete a variety of activities designed to heighten their awareness of the organizational scheme of the library and its resources.

STRATEGIES:
1. Students need to become aware that the library contains a vast amount of information. By becoming familiar with the library's layout and its various resources, they can have access to much information.

2. Once a library skill has been taught, it is important that students are given the opportunity to practice the skill on a regular basis. Otherwise, these skills will be lost.

3. Library skills are best learned when students have a real need to obtain some information. When students have a purpose for learning a skill, they are more likely to remember the skill for the future.

4. With the operations of libraries expanding all the time, it is not realistic that students will be able to learn every aspect of library operation. The most important lesson we can teach students is that the library is a tremendous resource. Librarians are there to help students gain access to information they need. It is important that we encourage students to ask questions and learn how to use the library for solving whatever problems face them both now and in the future.

ANSWERS:
IIIB-3　What's in a Card Catalog?

1-2.	Author Card	Subject Card	Title Card
	+	+	+
	+	+	+
	+	+	+
	−	+	−
	+	+	+
	+	+	+
	+	+	+
	−	−	−

4. Be sure to have students note differences besides the fact that the author and title cards do not list the subject. The order of information on the card is the main difference that should be discussed.

IIIB-5　How to Use The Readers' Guide to Periodical Literature *I*

Entry 1:　a. What's so great about CBS News?

　　　　　b. Fortune

　　　　　c. D. Seligman

　　　　　d. 114

e. 127-8

f. October 27, 1986

g. none

Entry 2: a. Tune into turning off TV

b. Teen

c. not listed

d. 30

e. 64

f. August 1986

g. il (meaning "illustrated")

Entry 3: a. Tuning in children's books

b. Publisher's Weekly

c. E. Klavan

d. 230

e. 28-31

f. September 26, 1986

g. il (meaning "illustrated")

IIIB-6 How to Use The Readers' Guide to Periodical Literature *II*
1. four; boldface type and the major topics are out to the left of the entries
2. eight; TV makes the reader [Reading Rainbow series]
3. four; H. Friedman
4. Television and youth; Youth in the television industry
5. N.Y. Times Book Review; 91; 7/27/86; 22

IIIB-9 What Does a Map Help Us to Know?
1. the United States
2. a. Eggs and Poultry
   b. Potatoes
   c. Manufacturing
3. Gulf of Mexico; Atlantic Ocean; Pacific Ocean
4. 250
5. a. Oregon
   b. Snake River
   c. tobacco
   d. ++++++
   e. yes

WHERE IS EVERYTHING IN THE LIBRARY?

OBJECTIVE: Drawing a floor plan of the library

MATERIALS: For this activity, you will need a sheet of plain white or graph paper, a pencil, and a ruler.

PROCEDURE:

1. Draw the perimeter of the library on your paper.

2. Take note of the location of the following items in the library:

card catalog	short stories
check-out desk	globes
periodicals (magazines and newspapers)	media center (computers, microfiche machines, videos, etc.)
reference books	
fiction books	student work areas
nonfiction books	any other notable areas
biographies	entrance and exit

3. Once you have located each of these areas, begin to place them into the rough draft map of the library. Use a symbol of some type to designate each area and be sure to include a legend or key to indicate what each symbol represents. The symbols could be pictures, letters, numbers, or colors.

4. Once you have all of the information that you need on your rough map, you can then make a final copy of the library map using a ruler.

WHAT'S IN A LIBRARY?

OBJECTIVE: Searching the library for information

MATERIALS: For this activity, you will need a pencil.

PROCEDURE: In order to become familiar with some of the information in the library, you will work with a partner in completing the following information hunt. Working together, you are to find the following information and fill in the correct data. Each of you will fill in your own form.

1. Write the title and author of a fiction book whose author's last name begins with the letter B.

   Title: _____

   Author: _____

2. For any encyclopedia, find this information.

   Title: _____

   Publishing company: _____

   City of publication: _____

   Copyright year: _____

3. For a biography, identify the following information.

   Title: _____

   Author: _____

   Subject of book: _____

4. Locate a book on sharks and identify the following information.

   Title: _____

   Author: _____

   Number of pages: _____   Call number: _____

WHAT'S IN A LIBRARY? (continued)

5. Locate the current year's almanac. Find information about a natural disaster.

Disaster: _____

When it happened? _____

Where it happened? _____

Death toll or other effects: _____

6. Locate an atlas that contains a map of the ocean floor. The Mariana Trench is lo-

cated in the _____ Ocean and its depth is _____ feet below sea level.

7. Locate *The Readers' Guide to Periodical Literature.* Draw a rough sketch of the library's floor plan on the back of this sheet and indicate on the map where this series of books is located.

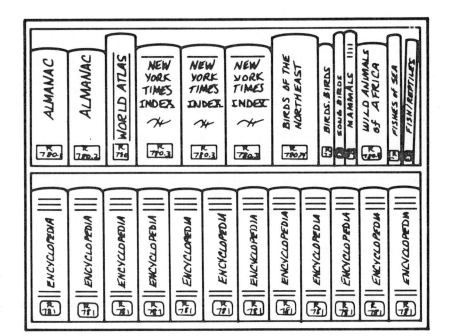

Name _____ Date _____

WHAT'S IN A CARD CATALOG?

OBJECTIVE: Examining the similarities and differences among the author, subject, and title cards found in the library's card catalog

MATERIALS: For this activity, you will need the author/subject/title cards handout and a pencil.

PROCEDURE:

1.   On the handout are three sample card catalog cards: the author card, the subject card, and the title card. Examine the author card first. Indicate on the chart below whether the card contains the following information by using a + for "yes" and a − for "no."

Information	Author Card	Subject Card	Title Card
book title	_____	_____	_____
book's author	_____	_____	_____
call number	_____	_____	_____
subject	_____	_____	_____
publisher	_____	_____	_____
date of publication	_____	_____	_____
number of pages	_____	_____	_____

2.   Now do the same for the subject and title cards.

3.   Once you have completed this information, examine how the three cards are the same and how they are different.

4.   From your observations, what are the differences among these three cards?

_____

_____

_____

Author Card

```
793.8      Abbamont, Gary
              The great bicycle race/
           by Gary Abbamont, with Heidi
           Hoover.—New York: Quality
           Books, 1990.
                 341 p.: ill. (col.)
                 Bibliography: p. 336
```

Subject Card

```
793.8      BICYCLES
              by Gary Abbamont, with
           Heidi Hoover/The great bicycle
           race.—New York: Quality
           Books, 1990.
                 341 p.: ill. (col.)
                 Bibliography: p. 336
```

Title Card

```
793.8      The great bicycle race
              by Gary Abbamont, with
           Heidi Hoover/The great bicycle
           race.—New York: Quality
           Books, 1990.
                 341 p.: ill. (col.)
                 Bibliography: p. 336
```

HOW TO USE THE CARD CATALOG

OBJECTIVE: Locating two or more books by the same author or on the same subject

MATERIALS: For this activity, you will need a pencil.

PROCEDURE: Using the card catalog, you are to locate either two books by the same author OR two books on the same subject. Then fill in the information below for each book.

BOOK 1

Title: _____

Author: _____

Publisher: _____

Date of publication: _____ Call number: _____ Number of pages: _____

BOOK 2

Title: _____

Author: _____

Publisher: _____

Date of publication: _____ Call number: _____ Number of pages: _____

HOW TO USE *THE READERS' GUIDE TO PERIODICAL LITERATURE* I

OBJECTIVE: Understanding a *Readers' Guide* entry
MATERIALS: For this activity, you will need a pencil.
PROCEDURE: Study the following *Readers' Guide* entry. Then identify the specific parts of this and the next two entries.

ENTRY 1:   What's so great about CBS News? D. Seligman. *Fortune*
               114:127-8 O 27 '86

a. Article's title: _____

b. Magazine's title: _____

c. Author of article: _____

d. Volume number: _____

e. Page number(s): _____

f. Date of magazine: _____

g. Other information and abbreviations: _____

ENTRY 2:   Tune into turning off TV. il *Teen* 30:64 Ag '86

a. Article's title: _____

b. Magazine's title: _____

c. Author of article: _____

d. Volume number: _____

e. Page number(s): _____

f. Date of magazine: _____

g. Other information and abbreviations: _____

HOW TO USE *THE READERS' GUIDE* (continued)

ENTRY 3:   Tuning in children's books. E. Klavan. il *Publ Wkly*
230:28–31 S 26 '86

a.   Article's title: _____

b.   Magazine's title: _____

c.   Author of article: _____

d.   Volume number: _____

e.   Page number(s): _____

f.   Date of magazine: _____

g.   Other information and abbreviations: _____

Name _____ Date _____

HOW TO USE *THE READERS' GUIDE TO PERIODICAL LITERATURE* II

OBJECTIVE: Reading a sample section from *Readers' Guide*

MATERIALS: For this activity, you will need a pencil.

PROCEDURE: Use the following sample section from the *Readers' Guide* to answer the questions. The sample section relates to the subject of television, and is reprinted here with permission of The H. W. Wilson Company, copyright © 1986.

1. How many major topics relating to television are shown in this sample?

   _____ How does the *Readers' Guide* help

   you to see these major topics? _____

   _____

   _____

2. Under the topic of "Television and Reading," how many entries are listed?

   _____ What is the title of the seventh

   entry under this topic? _____

   _____

   _____

3. Under the topic "Television and the Deaf," how many entries are listed?

   _____ Who is the author of the article titled "Closed-Captioning"? _____

Television and reading
Book characters on TV interest children to read. *Jet* 70:36 Je 30 '86
Burton's 'Reading rainbow' is peaking kids' interest. il *Jet* 70:22 Jl 7 '86
Heads Up for literacy [Sing, Spell, Read & Write program at the Christian Broadcasting Network] H. G. Miller. il *Saturday Evening Post* 258:50-1+ S '86
Reading rainbow: a handful of new approaches to children's books and other media. D. E. Roback. bibl il *Publ W'kly* 229:50 Mr 21 '86
Reading, writing and rationality [views of N. Postman] G. F. Will. il *Newsweek* 107:86 Mr 17 '86
TV defender squishes bookworms [excerpt from Television today and tomorrow] C. Dunkley. *Channels Commun* 5:79 Ja/F '86
TV makes the reader [Reading rainbow series] T. Lewin. *N Y Times Book Rev* 91:22 Jl 27 '86
Two TV networks unite to promote literacy [ABC and PBS] H. Fields. *Publ Wkly* 229:20 Ja 17 '86
Television and the aged
Nebraska ETV's "Grand generations". B. L. Curry. il por *Aging* no354:10-12 '86
Television and the deaf
Closed-caption costs spark debate between 'Cosby' producers, NBC. *Jet* 69:56 Ja 27 '86
Closed-caption decoder (I). J. D. Gifford. il *Radio-Electron* 57:41-5 N '86
Closed-caption decoder (II). J. D. Gifford. il *Radio-Electron* 57:61-4 D '86
Closed-captioning. H. Friedman. il *Radio-Electron* 57:92+ O '86
Television and youth
    See also
    Youth in the television industry
Education, television, and political discourse in America [interview with G. Anastaplo] D. McDonald. por *Cent Mag* 19:20-6 Jl/Ag '86

4. Sometimes a "See also" label is used under the topic heading. This lets you know that there is another topic that you can look up in order to find articles on the topic. Which

   topic in this sample has a "See also" entry? _____

   Under what other topic could you find information on this topic? _____

   _____

HOW TO USE *THE READERS' GUIDE* (continued)

5. In what magazine will you find the article titled "TV Makes the Reader"?

_____

What is this magazine's volume number? _____What is this magazine's

date? _____ On what page (s) will you find this article? _____

Name _____ Date _____

WHAT'S IN *THE READERS' GUIDE TO PERIODICAL LITERATURE?*

OBJECTIVE: Locating articles for a given topic using *The Readers' Guide to Periodical Literature*

MATERIALS: For this activity, you will need the *Readers' Guide* and a pencil.

PROCEDURE:

1. Select a topic of current interest.
2. Using the *Readers' Guide,* locate five articles on this particular topic.
3. For each article you find, fill out the necessary information in the chart below.

TOPIC OF INTEREST: _____

ARTICLE'S TITLE	AUTHOR	MAGAZINE	DATE	VOLUME	PAGES

WHAT'S IN AN ALMANAC?

OBJECTIVE: Using an almanac to locate current information on a topic of interest and presenting the information in a form for others to see

MATERIALS: For this activity, you will need a current almanac, a pencil, paper, and a ruler.

PROCEDURE:

1. The almanac is a book that presents information on a variety of topics. It is updated each year and is valued for its current data. Take some time to look through the index located at the front of the book. You will see information on actors and actresses, crimes, best sellers, disasters, notable people, etc.

2. Select a natural disaster listed in the almanac. Look up information on this disaster.

3. Look at the sample chart below that shows one way to present information about a disaster.

TYPE OF DISASTER	DATE	LOCATION	CASUALTIES/DAMAGES
Flood	May 31, 1889	Johnstown, PA	2,200 died
Tropical storm	June 20, 1972	Eastern coast of U.S.	129 died 115,000 homeless $3.5 billion in damages

4. Design a chart that you can use to present the information you have selected. Fill in the chart and be prepared to share your results with the class. Be sure to give your chart a title.

EXTENSION: Select another topic of interest to you. Locate the information on the topic, design a chart to present your data, and complete the chart for your classmates to read.

WHAT DOES A MAP HELP US TO KNOW?

OBJECTIVE: Using an atlas to interpret information
MATERIALS: For this activity, you will need the map handout, a pencil, and a ruler.
PROCEDURE: Using the map handout, fill in the following missing information.

1. This map shows the country of _____ .

2. In the lower left corner of this map is a LEGEND. This legend tells us what the pictures or symbols on the map mean. What does each of the following symbols mean?

    a. _____

    b. _____

    c. _____

3. In the bottom right corner is a COMPASS. This tells us which direction is north on the map. On this map, the north points up. What body of water is south of the United

    States? _____

    What body of water is east of the United States? _____

    What body of water is west of the United States? _____

4. Below the legend of the map is a SCALE. This scale helps us to estimate distances on the map. This map has two scales: one in kilometers and one in miles. About how many miles are there between the cities of Houston and Dallas in Texas? Circle one: 250,   600,   or 1000

5. This map also shows us other information: state borders, water bodies, and land bodies. Try to answer the following questions:

    a. Which state is north of California?   _____

    b. What river passes south of Boise, Idaho?   _____

WHAT DOES A MAP HELP US TO KNOW? (continued)

c. What crop is grown in Virginia? _____

d. What symbol shows a railroad track? _____

e. Are any railroad tracks shown in _____
North Dakota?

EXTENSION: Using an atlas, select a map and develop a series of questions for a classmate to answer.

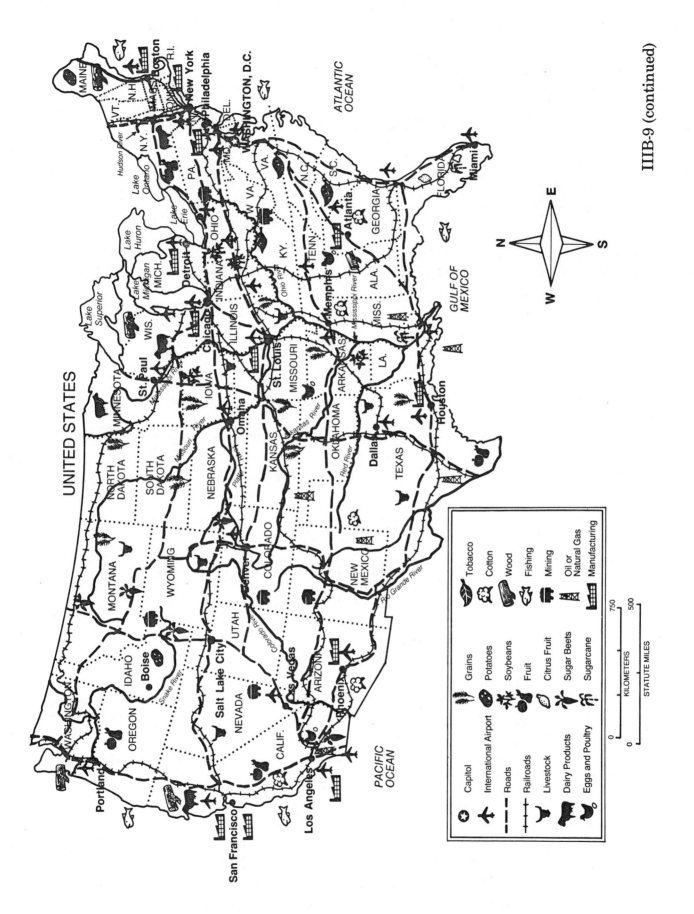

UNITED STATES

Legend:

Capitol	Grains	Tobacco	
International Airport	Potatoes	Cotton	
Roads	Soybeans	Wood	
Railroads	Fruit	Fishing	
Livestock	Citrus Fruit	Mining	
Dairy Products	Sugar Beets	Oil or Natural Gas	
Eggs and Poultry	Sugarcane	Manufacturing	

KILOMETERS
STATUTE MILES
0   500   750

IIIB-9 (continued)

WHAT'S IN AN ENCYCLOPEDIA?

OBJECTIVE: Using an encyclopedia to gather information about a specific topic
MATERIALS: For this activity, you will need encyclopedias and a pencil.
PROCEDURE: Using the encyclopedias, locate information on each of these sea creatures and record information for each category in the chart.

SEA CREATURE	PHYSICAL CHARACTERISTICS	FOOD-GETTING METHODS	DEFENSE MECHANISMS
Dolphin			
Octopus			
Shark			
Whale			

SKILL: C. Reading to Survive

OBJECTIVE:
Students will complete a variety of activities requiring them to locate information that is found in common, everyday materials. Students will develop skills required to read and use forms, telephone directories, newspapers, signs, maps, labels, and catalogs.

STRATEGIES:

1. Make students aware of the format or organization of the material used in each activity. Discuss the purpose of the material and how its purpose influences the format and organization of the material.
2. Help students become familiar with the terminology and general directions used in each type of material.
3. Students should be made aware of the importance of neatness and legibility when completing forms.

SPECIAL DIRECTIONS:
Make an overhead transparency of each form. Use the transparency to discuss the purpose of each form, its terminology, directions, and layout for group teaching. Have the students complete the form together as you discuss each item.

TEACHING HINTS:
"What's the Main Idea?" provides a basic form to help students read a news article and identify the main idea. The questions at the bottom of the page may be reproduced and used repeatedly with other readings.

ANSWERS:

IIIC-5 What's in a Weather Map?

1. a. 

   b. 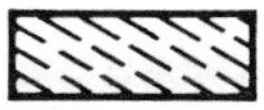

   c. 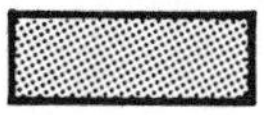
2. temperature is in the 30's, snowing
3. 50's
4. 40's
5. southeast; warmer temperatures
6. a variety of possible answers; have students give rationale for their responses

7. in the teens; northeast Maine

8. 80's; Florida

9. answers will vary

IIIC-12 What's So Funny?

1. the continent of Africa; starving people; the people in the world who have plenty of material goods

2. answers will vary

3. the starving child is holding an empty bowl while the two people with gifts in their hands are worrying about whom they might have forgotten to buy gifts for

4. answers will vary

5. answers will vary

IIIC-14 Can I Do the Job?

1. *Position:* Swimming pool service man's helper

   Qualifications: None

   Responsibilities: None listed

   Salary: $6 an hour and $50 bonus each month

   Hours: 40 hours plus overtime, seasonal

2. *Position:* Electrician

   Qualifications: Knowledge of traffic signals

   Responsibilities: Troubleshoot and maintain traffic signals; capable of working alone

   Salary: Not listed

   Hours: Not listed

3. *Position:* Chauffeur

   Qualifications: References required

   Responsibilities: None listed

   Salary: None listed

   Hours: Must be prepared to work flexible hours; shifts available 6 a.m.–2 p.m. and 5 p.m.–1 a.m.

4. *Position:* Plastics factory production worker

   Qualifications: None listed

   Responsibilities: Production work

   Salary: $6 an hour, overtime, benefits

   Hours: 12-hour shifts over a 3½-day work week

IIIC-15 What Does It Say?

1.	telephone	7.	duck crossing
2.	men's room	8.	restaurant
3.	information	9.	playground
4.	hospital	10.	construction
5.	picnic area	11.	falling rocks
6.	no left turn	12.	low bridge

IIIC-16 What Are the Parts of a Map?

1. on the moon
2. the Lunar Land Transportation Center
3. Crater Village Public School
4. space market
   hydroponic vegetable lab
   library
   public school

IIIC-17 Which Way Should I Go?

1. fire station
2. quiet—hospital zone
3. pedestrian crossing
4. playground
5. one-way street

IIIC-18 Where Do Signs Belong?

Have students give their rationale for placing their signs where they did.

IIIC-20 How Should That Medicine Be Used?

1. fever and discomfort due to colds, flu, simple pain, teething, immunizations, and tonsillectomy
2. 4 tablets
3. 5
4. 4 hours
5. contact a physician or poison control center immediately
6. a. if fever persists for more than 3 days
   b. if pain continues for more than 5 days
   c. if the patient takes an overdosage of the medication
7. have students offer rationales for their responses to this question

IIIC-21 What Should I Know When Using Household Cleaners?

1. wash thoroughly with soap and large quantities of water, then cover with moist magnesia or baking soda
2. cause a burn
3. flush with large amounts of water and get prompt medical attention
4. hydrochloric acid

5. in original container in areas inaccessible to small children, and away from heat or open flame in a well-ventilated area away from food or feed

6. no

IIIC-22 What Am I Eating?

Serving Size: 1 ounce (1¼ cups)

Calories: 110

Grams of Protein: 4; 6

Grams of Carbohydrate: 20; none listed

Grams of Fat: 2; none listed

Vitamins: A; 25

C; 25

D; 10

IIIC-27 How Much Does Money Cost?

1. $88.85   4. $300.30

2. $91.68   5. $1066.20

3. $15.43

IIIC-28 What's on TV?

1. the movie *Rio Lobo*

2. 7:30

3. New York Knicks and Boston Celtics

4. Channel 2 at 7:00

Channel 4 at 7:00

Channel 5 at 7:00 and 10:00

Channel 9 at 10:00

Channel 11 at 7:30

Channel 13 at 7:30

5. Chef Louis and Metro Report

6. Dallas

WHAT ARE THE PARTS OF A FORM?

OBJECTIVE: Reading forms

MATERIALS: For this activity, you will need a pencil.

PROCEDURE: Fill in this form with the requested information. Read carefully and follow directions exactly.

<table>
<tr><td colspan="2">U.S. Postal Service
CHANGE OF ADDRESS ORDER</td><td colspan="3">Customer Instructions: Complete Items 1 thru 9. Except Item 8, please PRINT all information including address on face of card.</td><td colspan="2">**OFFICIAL USE ONLY**</td></tr>
<tr><td colspan="5">1. Change of Address for *(Check one)* ☐ Individual   ☐ Entire Family   ☐ Business</td><td colspan="2">Zone/Route ID No.</td></tr>
<tr><td colspan="2">2. Start Date Month Day Year</td><td colspan="3">If TEMPORARY address, print
3. date to discontinue forwarding   Month Day Year</td><td colspan="2">Date Entered on Form 3982
M M D D Y Y</td></tr>
<tr><td colspan="5">4. <u>Print</u> Last Name or Name of Business *(If more than one, use separate Change of Address Order Form for each)*</td><td colspan="2">Expiration Date
M M D D Y Y</td></tr>
<tr><td colspan="5">5. <u>Print</u> First Name of Head of Household *(include Jr., Sr., etc.)*. Leave blank if the Change of Address Order is for a business.</td><td colspan="2">Clerk/Carrier Endorsement</td></tr>
<tr><td colspan="7">6. <u>Print</u> **OLD** mailing address, number and street *(if Puerto Rico, include urbanization zone)*</td></tr>
<tr><td colspan="7">Apt./Suite No.   P.O. Box No.   R.R/HCR No.   Rural Box/HCR Box No.</td></tr>
<tr><td colspan="7">City   State   ZIP Code</td></tr>
<tr><td colspan="7">7. <u>Print</u> **NEW** mailing address, number and street *(if Puerto Rico, include urbanization zone)*</td></tr>
<tr><td colspan="7">Apt./Suite No.   P.O. Box No.   R.R/HCR No.   Rural Box/HCR Box No.</td></tr>
<tr><td colspan="7">City   State   ZIP Code</td></tr>
<tr><td colspan="3">8. Signature *(See conditions on reverse)*</td><td colspan="4" rowspan="3">**OFFICIAL USE ONLY**</td></tr>
<tr><td colspan="3">9. Date Signed   Month Day Year</td></tr>
<tr><td colspan="3">**OFFICIAL USE ONLY**
Verification Endorsement</td></tr>
</table>

PS Form 3575, Mar. 1988   ✿U.S.G.P.O. 1989 231-597

HOW CAN I GET A PASSPORT?

OBJECTIVE: Completing a form for a U.S. passport

MATERIALS: For this activity, you will need the sample passport form and a pencil.

PROCEDURE: Read carefully and follow the directions exactly. Fill in the form with the requested information.

UNITED STATES DEPARTMENT OF STATE
APPLICATION FOR ☐ PASSPORT ☐ REGISTRATION
SEE INSTRUCTIONS—TYPE OR PRINT IN INK IN WHITE AREAS

1. NAME FIRST NAME   MIDDLE NAME

LAST NAME

2. MAILING ADDRESS

STREET

CITY, STATE,
ZIP CODE

COUNTRY   IN CARE OF

☐ 5 Yr.   ☐ 10 Yr.   Issue
Date _____

R   D   O   DP

End. # _____   Exp. _____

3. SEX   **4. PLACE OF BIRTH** City, State or Province, Country   **5. DATE OF BIRTH**   **6. SEE FEDERAL TAX** SOCIAL SECURITY NUMBER
LAW NOTICE ON
REVERSE SIDE

Male   Female   Mo.   Day   Year

7. HEIGHT   **8. COLOR OF HAIR**   **9. COLOR OF EYES**   **10. (Area Code) HOME PHONE**   **11. (Area Code) BUSINESS PHONE**

Feet Inches   **12. PERMANENT ADDRESS (Street, City, State, ZIP Code)**   **13. OCCUPATION**

FOLD

14. FATHER'S NAME   BIRTHPLACE   BIRTH DATE   U.S. CITIZEN   **16. TRAVEL PLANS** *(Not Mandatory)*
☐ YES ☐ NO   COUNTRIES   DEPARTURE DATE

15. MOTHER'S MAIDEN NAME   BIRTHPLACE   BIRTH DATE   U.S. CITIZEN
☐ YES ☐ NO   LENGTH OF STAY

17. HAVE YOU EVER BEEN ISSUED A U.S. PASSPORT?   YES ☐   NO ☐   IF YES, SUBMIT PASSPORT IF AVAILABLE.   ☐ Submitted
IF UNABLE TO SUBMIT MOST RECENT PASSPORT, STATE ITS DISPOSITION: COMPLETE NEXT LINE
NAME IN WHICH ISSUED   PASSPORT NUMBER   ISSUE DATE (Mo., Day, Yr.)   DISPOSITION

SUBMIT TWO RECENT
IDENTICAL PHOTOS

2" × 2"   FROM 1" TO 1-3/8"

18. HAVE YOU EVER BEEN MARRIED? ☐ YES   ☐ NO   DATE OF MOST
RECENT MARRIAGE   Mo.   Day   Year

WIDOWED/DIVORCED?   ☐ YES   ☐ NO   IF YES, GIVE DATE   Mo.   Day   Year

SPOUSE'S FULL BIRTH NAME   SPOUSE'S BIRTHPLACE

19. IN CASE OF EMERGENCY, NOTIFY *(Person Not Traveling With You)*   RELATIONSHIP
(Not Mandatory)
FULL NAME

ADDRESS   (Area Code) PHONE NUMBER

20. TO BE COMPLETED BY AN APPLICANT WHO BECAME A CITIZEN THROUGH NATURALIZATION
I IMMIGRATED TO THE U.S.   I RESIDED CONTINUOUSLY IN THE U.S.   DATE NATURALIZED (Mo., Day, Yr.)
(Month, Year)   From (Mo., Yr.)   To (Mo., Yr.)

PLACE

21. DO NOT SIGN APPLICATION UNTIL REQUESTED TO DO SO BY PERSON ADMINISTERING OATH
I have not, since acquiring United States citizenship, performed any of the acts listed under "Acts or Conditions" on the reverse of this application form (unless explanatory statement is attached). I solemnly swear (or affirm) that the statements made on this application are true and the photograph attached is a true likeness of me.

Subscribed and sworn to (affirmed) before me   (SEAL)   X _____

Month Day Year

☐ Clerk of Court or
☐ PASSPORT Agent
☐ Postal Employee   *(Sign in presence of person authorized to accept application)*
☐ (Vice) Consul USA At _____

(Signature of person authorized to accept application)

22. APPLICANT'S IDENTIFYING DOCUMENTS ☐ PASSPORT ☐ DRIVER'S ☐ OTHER (Specify)
       LICENSE
ISSUE DATE   EXPIRATION DATE   No.
       PLACE OF ISSUE   ISSUED IN THE NAME OF
Month Day Year   Month Day Year

23. FOR ISSUING OFFICE USE ONLY (Applicant's evidence of citizenship)

☐ Birth Cert.   SR   CR   City   Filed/Issued:
☐ Passport   Bearer's Name:
☐ Report of Birth
☐ Naturalization/Citizenship Cert.   No.:
☐ Other:
☐ Seen &
Returned
☐ Attached

APPLICATION APPROVAL

Examiner Name

Office, Date

24.

FEE _____ EXEC. _____ POST _____

FORM DSP-11 (12–87)   (SEE INSTRUCTIONS ON REVERSE)   Form Approved OMB No. 1405-0004 (Exp. 8/1/89)

IIIC-2 (continued)

HOW CAN I GET A JOB?

OBJECTIVE: Completing a job application

MATERIALS: For this activity, you will need the sample job application and a pen.

PROCEDURE:

1. Fill in the form with the requested information as if you are actually applying for the position assigned by your teacher. Your application will be evaluated along with others from your class before a decision is reached as to who will get the position.

2. You are to print in ink.

3. Be sure to read carefully and follow the directions exactly.

Name _____ Date _____

JOB APPLICATION

Position Desired _____ Date _____

PERSONAL INFORMATION

Name _____ Address _____
     Last   First   M.I.   Street

Telephone ( ) _____
                                   City   State   Zip

EDUCATION

High School	Address	Dates Attended	Date Graduated	Degree

Higher Education	Address	Dates Attended	Date Graduated	Degree

EXPERIENCE   List most recent experience first.

Position	Employer	Address	Dates of Employment	Reason for Leaving

REFERENCES   List 3 references.

Name	Position	Address	Telephone

PERSONAL STATEMENT

1. What qualities do you possess which make you the most desirable candidate for this position?

2. Why do you want this position?

3. How will this position help you to attain your career goals?

© 1990 by The Center for Applied Research in Education

Name _____ Date _____

WHAT'S THE NUMBER?

OBJECTIVE: Locating information in a telephone directory

MATERIALS: For this activity, you will need the telephone directory handout, a pencil, and a local telephone directory.

PROCEDURE: Use your local telephone directory to find the information requested. The following hints may be helpful when using the telephone directory.

- All listings are in alphabetical order.

- Look for the page by using the key name listings at the top of the page. They show the first and last names on each page.

- Look across the top of each column to see in which column the name should appear.

- Initials are listed before first names. For example, Doe J. would be before Doe John.

- Abbreviations are listed alphabetically as if the words were spelled out. For example, St. Louis is listed as if it were spelled Saint Louis.

- Numbers used as names are listed alphabetically as if the numbers were spelled out. For example, 299 Shop is listed as if it were Two Nine Nine Shop.

- Letters used as names are at the beginning of the listings of that letter. For example, R & L Institute is listed at the beginning of R.

- Names may be listed in different ways. For example, John Doe Company might be listed under J for John or under D for Doe. Be sure of the spelling—it could be John Doah Company or John Dough Company. It helps to have the address.

Name _____ Date _____

TELEPHONE DIRECTORY HANDOUT

1. Write in the telephone numbers you would dial in case of an emergency:

   Police: _____

   Fire: _____

   Ambulance: _____

   State Police: _____

   Poison Control Center: _____

   Gas Company Service Department: _____

   State Child Abuse Control: _____

   Federal Bureau of Investigation (FBI): _____

   Telephone Business Office: _____

   Mayor's Office:_____

2. Write in the area code for each of the following places:

   Los Angeles, California: _____

   Florida: _____

   New York City: _____

   Washington, D.C.: _____

   Montana: _____

   Your Town: _____

3. Write in the telephone numbers for the following:

   Time: _____

   Weather: _____

4. When do you need to use an area code:

   _____

   _____

TELEPHONE DIRECTORY HANDOUT (continued)

5. What time of day is it least expensive to call long distance?

    _____

6. What is the difference between "Dial Direct" and "Operator Assisted" calls?

    _____

    _____

    _____

7. What is an 800 number?

    _____

8. What is the number for directory assistance in San Diego, California?

    _____

WHAT'S IN A WEATHER MAP?

OBJECTIVE: Locating information on a newspaper weather map
MATERIALS: For this activity, you will need the weather map handout and a pencil.
PROCEDURE: Use the weather map to answer the questions.

1. Look at the legend on the map. What are the symbols for the following:

    a. rain _____

    b. showers _____

    c. snow _____

2. Find Kansas City on the map. What can you tell about the weather for this city? ____
    _____

3. What is the temperature in San Francisco? _____

4. What is the temperature in Chicago? _____

5. Where on the map would you go to swim at the beach? _____
    Why? _____

6. Where on the map would you go to ski? _____
    Why? _____

7. What is the lowest temperature on the map? _____
    Where? _____

8. What is the highest temperature on the map? _____
    Where? _____

9. What is the temperature where you live? _____

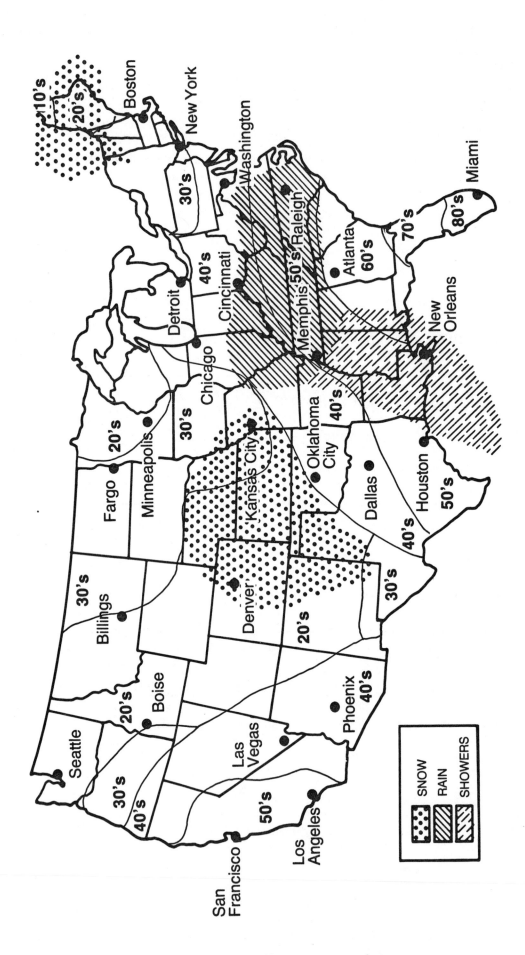

Name _____ Date _____

WHAT'S THE TEMPERATURE?

OBJECTIVE: Locating and presenting information in a newspaper weather map

MATERIALS: For this activity, you will need local newspaper weather maps for five consecutive days, graph paper, and a colored pencil or marker.

PROCEDURE:

1. Cut out your local newspaper weather map for five consecutive days.
2. Each day, write the date and the temperature for your area.
3. Put the information on the sample graph below.
4. Use the graph paper to make a final temperature graph.

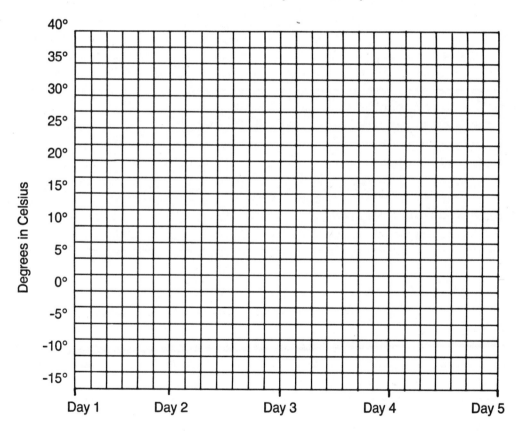

Temperature Graph

WHAT'S THE MAIN IDEA (I)?

OBJECTIVE: Reading a news article to identify the main idea
MATERIALS: For this activity, you will need a news article and a pencil.
PROCEDURE: (1) Read a news article. (2) Answer the following questions. (3) Write a
             sentence that includes the answers to these questions. NOTE: Not all
             questions will be answered in every article.

1. WHO is the article about?

   _____

   _____

2. WHAT happened?

   _____

   _____

   _____

3. WHEN did it happen?

   _____

4. WHERE did it happen?

   _____

5. HOW or WHY did it happen?

   _____

   _____

   _____

Main idea sentence:

   _____

   _____

   _____

WHAT'S THE MAIN IDEA (II)?

OBJECTIVE: Reading a news article to locate the main idea and identify details

MATERIALS: For this activity, you will need a news article and two different colored pencils.

PROCEDURE:

1. Read a news article.

2. Use a colored pencil to underline the words in the article that answer the following questions: WHO? WHAT? WHEN? WHERE? HOW? WHY? These words make up the main idea of the article.

3. Use another colored pencil to underline words that give other important details.

WHAT'S THE BEST PRICE?

OBJECTIVE: Locating and comparing prices for items in newspaper ads

MATERIALS: For this activity, you will need newspapers, scissors, tape, markers, and posterboard.

PROCEDURE:

1. Look through newspaper ads for similar products from different stores. You may find food items, clothing, toys, electronic equipment, cars, or other goods.

2. Cut out at least four ads for one type of product. Be sure the ads specify the name of the product, the name of the store, and the price.

3. Tape the ads to a sheet of poster paper.

4. On another sheet of paper write all the comparisons you can make from the information you have gathered. Tell how the products may be different and what effect those differences may have on the performance and long-term value of the product.

5. Finally, write which product you would buy and explain why.

WHAT DOES IT MEAN?

OBJECTIVE: Locating information in news articles

MATERIALS: For this activity, you will need newspapers, scissors, tape, posterboard, and markers.

PROCEDURE:

1. Look through your local newspaper for a news article concerning an on-going controversial topic. Possible topics include proposed laws, local zoning ordinances, candidates for public office, and other local issues. Cut out and read the article. Tape the article to a sheet of paper and write the date. Use the information from the article to fill in the chart.

2. Every day for a week, find, cut out, and read additional newspaper articles on the same topic. Tape each article to a sheet of paper and write the day's date. Then add the information on the chart.

3. Write an explanation of the issue. In the first paragraph explain the issue. In the second paragraph explain the major points on one side of the issue. In the third paragraph explain the major points on the other side of the issue. In the fourth paragraph write what you think should be done and why. Use information from the news articles to support your opinion.

WHAT SHOULD I WATCH?

OBJECTIVE: Locating TV listings and planning TV viewing time for one week

MATERIALS: For this activity, you will need a weekly newspaper TV listing, a pencil, paper, and a ruler.

PROCEDURE:

1. Look through the TV shows offered for one week. Choose the shows you would most like to watch. For this assignment, you should average no more than two hours of TV each day.

2. Make a chart like the one shown here. Fill in the information for your selected shows.

Chart for TV Viewing

Show Watched and Time	Mon	Tue	Wed	Thu	Fri	Sat	Sun

3. During the week, fill in your evaluation of each show you watch.

4. Then answer the following questions.

What kinds of TV shows do you like most? Why?

_____

_____

_____

How does TV fit into your daily schedule?

_____

_____

_____

WHAT SHOULD I WATCH? (continued)

What do you most like about TV?

_____

_____

_____

What do you most dislike about TV?

_____

_____

_____

Is it worthwhile to choose TV shows ahead of time? Why?

_____

_____

_____

Name _____ Date _____

WHAT'S SO FUNNY?

OBJECTIVE: Reading and analyzing a political cartoon
MATERIALS: For this activity, you will need a pencil.
PROCEDURE: A political cartoon uses symbols or satire to point out a topic of public
             interest. Political cartoons have a message. Look at the cartoon and
             answer the questions. (NOTE: This cartoon is an adaptation of one that
             appeared in London's *The Observer*.)

1. The child's shadow is symbolic. What do you think the shadow represents? _____

    _____

    Who does the child represent? _____

    _____ Who do the other people represent? _____

    _____

WHAT'S SO FUNNY? (continued)

2. In your own words, explain how the words in the cartoon explain the symbols. _____

_____

_____

_____

3. Describe the action taking place. _____

_____

_____

_____

4. Explain the message of the cartoon. _____

_____

_____

_____

5. What special interest groups would agree or disagree with the cartoon's message? Why? _____

_____

_____

_____

_____

_____

_____

WHAT DO I NEED?

OBJECTIVE: Using the classified section and newspaper ads

MATERIALS: For this activity, you will need newspapers, scissors, paper, and a pencil.

PROCEDURE:

1. Imagine that you have just found your first real job. You look at your finances and estimate that you have $2,500 to spend on furnishing the one-bedroom apartment shown below.

2. Make a list by room of all the things you will need to buy in order to live in your new apartment.

3. Look through newspaper advertisements and classified sections to find the things you will need. As you shop, cut out the ads you wish to use.

4. Add your purchases and adjust them to stay within your $2,500 budget.

5. On a sheet of paper, list the items you wish to purchase, the price of each item, and your total expenditure.

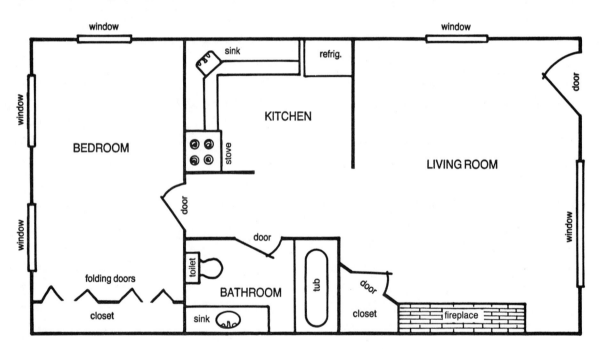

© 1990 by The Center for Applied Research in Education

Name _____ Date _____

CAN I DO THE JOB?

OBJECTIVE: Reading help wanted ads
MATERIALS: For this activity, you will need a pencil.
PROCEDURE: Read each of the following help wanted ads. Complete the chart. Some
ads may not supply all the information listed in the chart.

HELP WANTED AD	POSITION	QUALIFICATIONS	RESPONSIBILITIES	SALARY	HOURS
SWIMMING POOL Service Man's helpers to start immediately. Experience not necessary. Full time, seasonal. 40 hours a week plus OT. $6 an hour. $50 bonus each month employed.					
ELECTRICIAN Trouble shooting and maintenance of traffic signals. Must be capable of working alone. Only personnel with full knowledge of traffic controls need apply. Apply in person. 9-5.					
CHAUFFEUR-Dynamic President of growing company requires: 2 Chauffeurs. Must be prepared to work flex. hrs. Shifts avail from 6AM-2PM & 5PM-1AM. Refs req'd.					
FACTORY Plastics manufacturer is now hiring for steady production work. 3½ day work week with 12 hour shifts. We offer $6 per hour, formal training, overtime and exceptional co. paid benefits. Car preferred. Call Mon-Sat,					

WHAT DOES IT SAY?

OBJECTIVE: Reading signs
MATERIALS: For this activity, you will need a pencil.
PROCEDURE: Signs use symbols instead of words. Try to read these signs. Write the answers next to the signs.

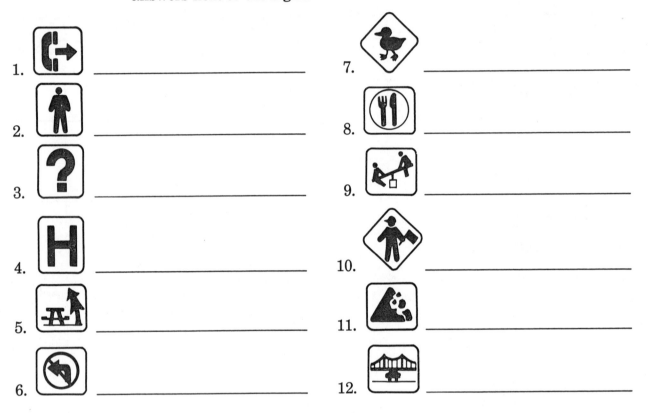

1. _____

2. _____

3. _____

4. _____

5. _____

6. _____

7. _____

8. _____

9. _____

10. _____

11. _____

12. _____

Name _____ Date _____

WHAT ARE THE PARTS OF A MAP?

OBJECTIVE: Reading a map

MATERIALS: For this activity, you will need the Crater Village Map, a ruler, and a pencil.

PROCEDURE: Use the Crater Village Map to fill in the following information.

1.   Where might Crater Village be located?

_____

2.   Look at the letters across the top and bottom of the map. Find the numbers along the sides of the map. These letters and numbers help you to locate things on the map.

Follow the lines to find the square C-4. What is located at C-4? _____

3.   Use the directional symbol to find what is located north of the Crater Village

Hydroponic Vegetable Lab. _____

4.   Follow these directions for a mystery tour of Crater Village: Begin your trip at the Lunar Land Transport Center. Head south and then west to get supplies at the

_____. Go east and then north to our space-age farm, the

_____. Then go northwest to borrow a tourist book at the

_____. Finally, go east to our educational facility, the _____

_____.

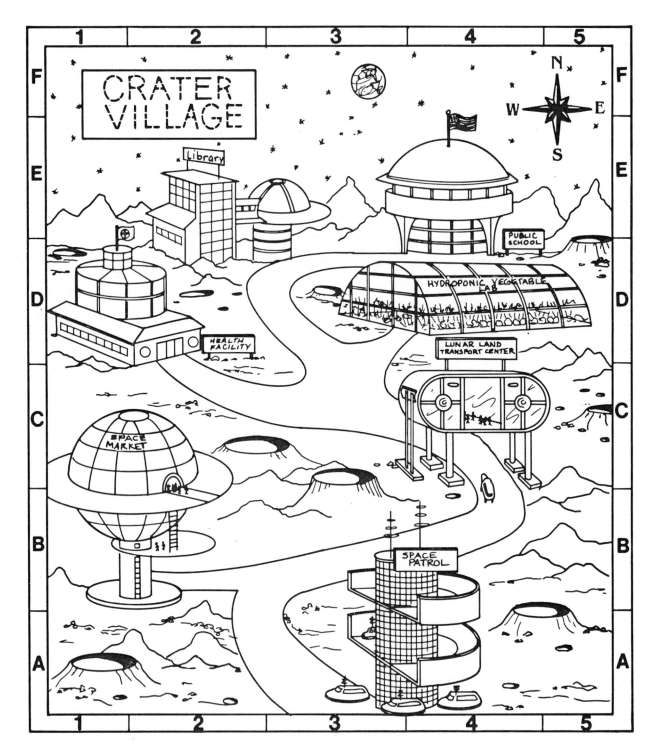

IIIC-16 (continued)

WHICH WAY SHOULD I GO?

OBJECTIVE: Reading a map and interpreting signs
MATERIALS: For this activity, you will need the neighborhood map and a pencil.
PROCEDURE: Look at the map and find the five signs. Write what each sign means.
                     Tell why the sign was placed in that particular location.

SIGN 1: _____

This sign is placed here because _____

_____

_____

SIGN 2: _____

This sign is placed here because _____

_____

_____

SIGN 3: _____

This sign is placed here because _____

_____

_____

SIGN 4: _____

This sign is placed here because _____

_____

_____

SIGN 5: _____

This sign is placed here because _____

_____

_____

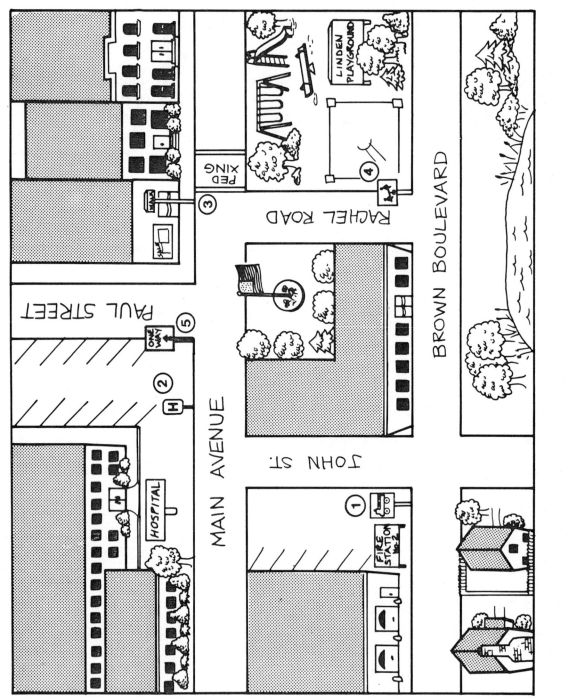

Name _____ Date _____

WHERE DO SIGNS BELONG?

OBJECTIVE: Reading a map

MATERIALS: For this activity, you will need a pencil.

PROCEDURE: Carefully study the map. Your job is to place signs in their appropriate locations. Draw the sign in its proper location and add it to the legend.

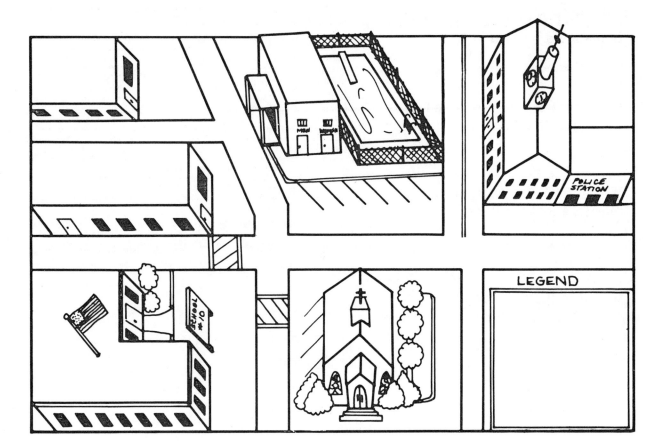

Name _____ Date _____

WHAT ARE THE PARTS OF A MEDICATION LABEL?

OBJECTIVE: Reading medication labels

MATERIALS: For this activity, you will need a pencil.

PROCEDURE: Look at the parts of the medication label below. Draw a line from each part listed to the same part on the medication label.

INDICATIONS (tells what medication should be used for)

DIRECTIONS (tells how much and how often to take it)

WARNING (tells important information about the drug)

INGREDIENTS (tells what is contained in the medication)

> **NO-SNEEZE   Decongestant Allergy Medication**
>
> **Indications:** Temporarily relieves nasal congestion, runny nose, sneezing, itching of the nose or throat, itchy, watery eyes due to hay fever or other upper respiratory allergies and runny nose, sneezing and nasal congestion of the common cold.
>
> **Directions:** Do not exceed recommended dosage because at higher doses nervousness, dizziness or sleeplessness may occur. Do not take this product for more than 7 days. If symptoms do not improve or are accompanied by fever, consult a physician. Do not take this product if you have heart disease, high blood pressure, thyroid disease, diabetes, asthma, glaucoma, emphysema, chronic pulmonary disease, shortness of breath, difficulty in breathing or difficulty in urination due to enlargement of the prostate gland unless directed by a physician. May cause excitability especially in children. May cause marked drowsiness; alcohol may increase the drowsiness effect. Avoid alcoholic beverages while taking this product. Use caution when driving a motor vehicle or operating machinery. Do not give this product to children under 12 years except under the advice and supervision of a physician. As with any drug, if you are pregnant or nursing a baby seek the advice of a health professional before using this product. Keep this and all drugs out of the reach of children. In case of accidental overdose, seek professional assistance or contact a Poison Control Center immediately.
>
> **Drug Interaction Precaution:** Do not take this product if you are presently taking a prescription drug for high blood pressure or depression without first consulting your physician.
>
> Each tablet contains Diphenhydramine HCl, USP) 25 mg. and Pseudoephedrine Hydrochloride 60 mg. Also contains: Corn Starch, Croscarmelose Sodium, Dibasic Calcium Phosphate Dihydrate, FD&C Blue No. 1 Aluminum Lake, Hydroxypropyl Methylcellulose, Microcrystalline Cellulose, Polyethylene Glycol, Polysorbate 80, Stearic Acid, Titanium Dioxide, and Zinc Stearate. **Store at room temperature 15°-30°C (59°-86°F). Protect from moisture.** See side panel or end flap for expiration date and lot number.

© 1990 by The Center for Applied Research in Education

Name _____ Date _____

HOW SHOULD THAT MEDICINE BE USED?

OBJECTIVE: Reading medication labels
MATERIALS: For this activity, you will need a pencil.
PROCEDURE: Use the label to complete the questions below.

Children's PAIN-AWAY Chewable Tablets

PAIN-AWAY is recommended by more doctors than any other brand of children's pain reliever for effective relief of fever and pain. PAIN-AWAY contains no aspirin and is unlikely to cause the serious side effects that may occur with aspirin in infants and young children dehydrated by fever. PAIN-AWAY is also unlikely to cause the stomach upset that may occur with aspirin, or to cause a reaction in those allergic to aspirin.

USAGE: For temporary relief of fever and discomfort due to colds and flu, and of simple pain and discomfort due to teething, immunizations and tonsillectomy.

DOSAGE: All dosages may be repeated every 4 hours, but not more than 5 times daily.

AGE (yr)	Under 2	2-3	4-5	6-8	9-10
WEIGHT (lb)	Under 24	24-35	36-47	48-59	60-71
TABLETS	Consult Physician	2	3	4	5

WARNING: Do not use if carton is opened or if a blister unit is broken. Keep this and all medication out of the reach of children. In case of accidental overdosage, contact a physician or poison control center immediately. Consult your physician if fever persists for more than three days or if pain continues for more than five days.

INACTIVE INGREDIENTS: Aspartame, Cellulose, Citric Acid, Ethyl-cellulose, Flavors, Magnesium Stearate, Mannitol, Starch, and Red #7.

---

1. For what symptoms should this medication be used?

    _____

    _____

    _____

    _____

2. How much of the medication should a 7-year-old child take?

    _____

3. How many dosages can be safely taken within a 24-hour period?

    _____

4. How much time must elapse between dosages?

    _____

HOW SHOULD THAT MEDICINE BE USED? (continued)

5. What should you do in case of an accidental overdosage?

   _____

   _____

6. For what three situations should you consult a physician?

   a. _____

   _____

   b. _____

   _____

   c. _____

   _____

7. If you were seven years old and weighed 65 pounds, what do you think you should do when trying to decide how much of the medication to take?

   _____

   _____

   _____

   _____

Name _____ Date _____

WHAT SHOULD I KNOW WHEN USING HOUSEHOLD CLEANERS?

OBJECTIVE: Reading labels on hazardous substances
MATERIALS: For this activity, you will need a pencil.
PROCEDURE: Use the label to answer the questions below.

SUDZO Toilet Bowl Cleaner

To Disinfect and Clean: Direct 4 oz. of powerful undiluted spray on the side of the bowl and under the rim, letting it run down into the water. Brush entire bowl, especially under the rim, the hard water ring and below the water line.

For Hard To Remove Stains: Squirt generous amount of Sudzo directly on stains. Let soak for 15 minutes before brushing. Do not close toilet lid. Close cap securely after each use. Rinse brush before putting away. Will not harm white or colored bowls. Will not harm plumbing. Sudzo has been specially formulated for use only in toilet bowls; it should not be used or placed on toilet lids, vanities, sinks, bathtubs, rugs, etc. **Do not use with chlorine bleach or any other chemical products.**
PRECAUTIONARY STATEMENTS:
HAZARDS TO HUMANS AND DOMESTIC ANIMALS
Danger: Corrosive—produces chemical burns. Contains Hydrochloric Acid. Do not get in eyes, on skin, or on clothing. May be fatal or harmful if swallowed. Do not breathe vapor or fumes. Keep out of reach of children.
First Aid: If swallowed, do not induce vomiting. Call a physician immediately. Drink large quantities of milk or water, followed by several tablespoonfuls of milk or water, followed by several tablespoonful of milk of magnesia or egg whites. Never give anything by mouth to an unconscious person. **IF IN EYES,** flush with large amounts of water and get prompt medical attention. **IF ON SKIN,** wash thoroughly with soap and large quantities of water, then cover with moist magnesia or baking soda.
Storage: Store in original container in areas inaccessible to small children. Keep securely closed away from heat or open flames in a well-ventilated area away from food or feed. Fumes are corrosive to metal.
Disposal: Do not reuse empty container. Rinse thoroughly with water and detergent. Discard in regular trash collection.

---

1. What should you do if you get some of the cleaner on your skin?

    _____

    _____

    _____

2. What will the product do to your skin?

    _____

WHAT SHOULD I KNOW WHEN USING HOUSEHOLD CLEANERS?
(continued)

3. What should you do if you get this cleaner in your eyes?

_____

_____

4. What is the hazardous ingredient in this product?

_____

5. How should this product be stored?

_____

_____

_____

_____

6. Can this product be safely mixed with other chemicals?

_____

Name _____ Date _____

WHAT AM I EATING?

OBJECTIVE: Reading a nutritional food label
MATERIALS: For this activity, you will need a pencil.
PROCEDURE: Use the nutrition information on this food label to complete the chart below.

NUTRITION INFORMATION PER SERVING

SERVING SIZE.. 1 OUNCE (1¼ CUPS)
SERVINGS PER PACKAGE 15

	1 ounce cereal
CALORIES	110
PROTEIN, GRAMS	4
CARBOHYDRATE, GRAMS	20
FAT, GRAMS	2
SODIUM, MILLIGRAMS..............	290

**PERCENTAGE OF U.S. RECOMMENDED
DAILY ALLOWANCES (U.S. RDA)**

PROTEIN	6
VITAMIN A	25
VITAMIN C	25
THIAMIN	25
RIBOFLAVIN	25
NIACIN	25
CALCIUM	4
IRON	45
VITAMIN D	10
VITAMIN B$_6$	25
VITAMIN B$_{12}$	25
PHOSPHORUS	10
MAGNESIUM	10
ZINC	6
COPPER...	4

INGREDIENTS: WHOLE OAT FLOUR, WHEAT STARCH, SUGAR, SALT, CALCIUM CARBONATE, TRISODIUM PHOSPHATE, VITAMIN C (SODIUM ASCORBATE), IRON (A MINERAL NUTRIENT), VITAMIN B (NIACIN), VITAMIN A (PALMITATE), VITAMIN B$_6$ (PYRIDOXINE HYDROCHLORIDE), VITAMIN B$_2$ (RIBOFLAVIN), VITAMIN B$_1$ (THIAMIN MONONITRATE), VITAMIN B$_{12}$, AND VITAMIN D.

	Amount Per Serving	% of U.S. Recommended Daily Allowance
Serving Size	_____	_____
Calories	_____	_____
Grams of Protein	_____	_____
Grams of Carbohydrate	_____	_____
Grams of Fat	_____	_____
Vitamin A		_____
Vitamin C		_____
Vitamin D		_____

WHAT'S IN MY FOOD?

OBJECTIVE: Reading the ingredients list from a food label

MATERIALS: For this activity, you will need a food label showing ingredients and a pencil.

PROCEDURE: Bring in a food label showing ingredients. Use this food label in order to complete the chart below. The ingredient contained in the greatest amount appears first in the list. The ingredients appear in descending order of their presence in the food. On the chart, list the ingredients in order. Then write a definition for each one and identify its source.

INGREDIENT	DEFINITION	SOURCE

© 1990 by The Center for Applied Research in Education

WHAT'S IN THE PACKAGE?

OBJECTIVE: Reading a food label
MATERIALS: For this activity, you will need a pencil and a food label.
PROCEDURE: Bring in a food label and answer each question below.

1. What is the name of the product?

_____

2. What is the net weight?

_____

3. Who makes the product?

_____

4. What are the ingredients in the product?

_____

_____

_____

_____

5. How many calories are in each serving?

_____

6. If the product is found to be unsatisfactory to the buyer, what does the company suggest the buyer do?

_____

_____

_____

Name _____ Date _____

HOW DO I ORDER FROM A CATALOG?

OBJECTIVE: Reading a catalog

MATERIALS: For this activity, you will need a mail order catalog and a pencil.

PROCEDURE: Use a mail order catalog to complete the order form below. Your order should include at least six different items totaling no more than $200.

SHOP-AT-HOME ORDER FORM

Please Print:

___Mrs.   ___Ms.

___Miss   ___Mr.   To send merchandise to another address:

My Name _____   Send to _____

My Address _____ Apt. _____   Address _____ Apt. _____

City/State _____ Zip _____   City/State _____ Zip _____

My Telephone # Is (___) _____

ITEM NUMBER (give complete correct no.)	HOW MANY?	ITEM NAME OR DESCRIPTION	SIZE	COLOR OR OTHER CHOICE	PAGE #	PRICE EACH	TOTAL	

TOTAL FOR MERCHANDISE		
SUBTOTAL		
SHIPPING & HANDLING		
Insurance: for 95¢, items lost or damaged in transit replaced free.		95¢
TOTAL		

SHIPPING & HANDLING CHART			
If order totals:	ADD:	If order totals:	ADD:
up to $15.00	2.95	$60.01 to $80	7.50
$15.01 to $25	3.95	$80.01 to $100	8.75
$25.01 to $40	4.95	over $100	9.50
$40.01 to $60	6.25		

WHAT'S THE BETTER VALUE?

OBJECTIVE: Comparison shopping using mail order catalogs

MATERIALS: For this activity, you will need a pencil and two mail order catalogs from different sources which contain similar merchandise.

PROCEDURE:

1. Choose an item from one catalog. Use the catalog to fill in the chart below for catalog 1.

2. Find a similar item in the other catalog. Then fill in the information for catalog 2.

3. Analyze the information in the chart to draw your conclusions.

CATALOG #	QUANTITY	PRODUCT	SIZE	COLOR	PRICE
1					
2					

CONCLUSIONS:

1. How are the items different in each catalog?

_____

_____

_____

2. How are the prices different in each catalog?

_____

_____

3. Which catalog would you use to purchase these items? Why?

_____

_____

_____

_____

Name _____ Date _____

HOW MUCH DOES MONEY COST?

OBJECTIVE: Reading a table to compute monthly loan payments

MATERIALS: For this activity, you will need a pencil.

PROCEDURE: The charge for borrowing money is called interest. Interest is charged on credit card accounts and loans of all kinds. The table below shows monthly payments for loans of $1000. Use the table to answer the questions.

This chart shows the approximate monthly payment for a loan of $1000 over varying periods of time and at varying interest rates. This can be used to compute the approximate monthly payment on any size loan. For example: For a $30,000 loan at 11.5% for 20 years, the approximate monthly payment would be $320.10. This figure is obtained by finding the payment for $1000 and multiplying by 30.

Months	10.0%	10.5%	11.0%	11.5%	12.0%	12.5%	13.0%	13.5%	14.0%	14.5%	15.0%	16%	17%	18%
12— 1 yr.	$87.92	$88.15	$88.39	$88.62	$88.85	$89.09	$89.32	$89.56	$89.79	$90.03	$90.26	$90.73	$91.20	$91.68
18— 1½ yr.	60.06	60.29	60.52	60.76	60.99	61.22	61.45	61.69	61.92	62.15	62.39	62.86	63.33	63.81
24— 2 yr.	46.15	46.38	46.61	46.85	47.08	47.31	47.55	47.78	48.02	48.25	48.49	48.96	49.44	49.92
30— 2½ yr.	37.82	38.05	38.28	38.52	38.75	38.99	39.23	39.46	39.70	39.94	40.18	40.66	41.15	41.64
36— 3 yr.	32.27	32.51	32.74	32.98	33.22	33.46	33.70	33.94	34.18	34.43	34.67	35.16	35.65	36.15
42— 3½ yr.	28.32	28.56	28.80	29.04	29.28	29.52	29.77	30.01	30.26	30.51	30.75	31.25	31.75	32.26
48— 4 yr.	25.37	25.61	25.85	26.09	26.34	26.58	26.83	27.08	27.33	27.58	27.84	28.34	28.85	29.38
60— 5 yr.	21.25	21.50	21.75	22.00	22.25	22.50	22.76	23.01	23.27	23.53	23.79	24.30	24.87	25.39
72— 6 yr.	18.53	18.78	19.04	19.30	19.56	19.82	20.08	20.34	20.61	20.88	21.15	21.67	22.27	22.81
84— 7 yr.	16.61	16.87	17.13	17.39	17.66	17.93	18.20	18.47	18.75	19.02	19.30	19.83	20.46	21.01
96— 8 yr.	15.18	15.45	15.71	15.98	16.26	16.53	16.81	17.09	17.38	17.66	17.95	18.50	19.14	19.72
108— 9 yr.	14.08	14.36	14.63	14.91	15.19	15.47	15.76	16.05	16.34	16.63	16.93	17.50	18.16	18.75
120— 10 yr.	13.22	13.50	13.78	14.06	14.35	14.64	14.94	15.23	15.53	15.83	16.14	16.73	17.41	18.02
180— 15 yr.	10.75	11.06	11.37	11.69	12.01	12.33	12.66	12.99	13.32	13.66	14.00	14.66	15.42	16.10
240— 20 yr.	9.66	9.99	10.33	10.67	11.02	11.37	11.72	12.08	12.44	12.80	13.17	13.88	14.70	15.43
300— 25 yr.	9.09	9.45	9.81	10.17	10.54	10.91	11.28	11.66	12.04	12.43	12.81	13.56	14.41	15.17
360— 30 yr.	8.78	9.15	9.53	9.91	10.29	10.68	11.07	11.46	11.85	12.25	12.65	13.42	14.28	15.07

© 1990 by The Center for Applied Research in Education

1. What is the monthly payment for a loan of $1,000 for one year at 12%? _____

2. What is the monthly payment for a loan of $1,000 for one year at 18%? _____

3. What is the monthly payment for a loan of $1,000 for 20 years at 18%? _____

4. What is the monthly payment for a loan of $5,000 for 18 months at 10%? _____

5. After making 12 monthly payments for a loan of $1,000 for one year at 12%, how much have you paid the lender? _____

Name _____ Date _____

WHAT'S ON TV?

OBJECTIVE: Reading a table of TV listings
MATERIALS: For this activity, you will need a pencil.
PROCEDURE: Use the table of TV listings to answer the questions below.

		7:00	7:30	8:00	8:30	9:00	9:30	10:00	10:30
2	News	Spin the Wheel	Comedy Special		Movie: "Muppets"				
4	News	Nova	Mystery Theater		Way of Life in US		Country Music Show	
5	News	Current Events	Movie: "Rio Lobo"				News	
7	Take a Chance	Tic Tac Toe	Aerobics	Chef Louis	Football: LA Raiders at Dallas Cowboys			
9	Building Blocks	Basketball: New York Knicks at Boston Celtics				News		
11	Yahoo	News	Sci Fi Stories		Movie: "Raiders of the Lost Ark"			
13	Business Reporter	News		Metro Report	Voyager		Political Review	

1. What show is on channel 5 at 8:00?

    _____

2. What time is the basketball game?

    _____

3. Which teams are playing in the basketball game?

    _____

WHAT'S ON TV? (continued)

4. List the times and channels for all the news shows.

_____

5. Which shows begin at 8:30?

_____

6. Where is the football game being played?

_____

unit IV

CONSTRUCTING GRAPHIC AIDS

Unit IV presents activities to help develop communication skills through constructing graphic aids. Traditionally in education, emphasis has been placed on written assignments. There is also a benefit in developing the student's ability to communicate in a variety of ways.

These activities are designed to make students aware of alternative methods of communicating information and to recognize the appropriateness and effectiveness of each. Students are directed in methods to construct pictures, diagrams, posters, tables, graphs, maps, and models.

Many benefits can be derived from an individual student's construction of graphic aids; however, there is much more to be gained through their subsequent use in the classroom as interesting, unusual, and highly motivational resources. The display of particularly effective graphic aids facilitates learning.

SKILL: A. Pictures, Diagrams, and Posters

OBJECTIVE:
Students will complete a variety of activities to help them develop their communication skills through the use of pictures, diagrams, and posters.

STRATEGIES:
1. Have students design a rough draft of the picture or diagram. This will allow the students to visualize and to organize the thoughts to be communicated. Discuss with students their use of different types, sizes, and colors of lettering. Large, bold lettering may be used to indicate greater importance whereas smaller lettering may indicate details.

2. It will be helpful to your students if you provide a set of directions/ checklists specific to the assignment. Assignments in graphic aids build upon student creativity. A self-evaluative checklist gives the student direction and parameters. The checklist also gives students the opportunity to evaluate their own work before it is evaluated by others. Each assignment you make will have its own requirements. Your direction/ checklist may direct students to include:

    *   title
    *   labeled parts
    *   vocabulary terms
    *   definitions of key terms
    *   illustrations (maps, portraits, diagrams, drawings, etc.)
    *   an explanation of the relationships among the parts
    *   interesting facts relating to the illustration
    *   appropriate lettering
    *   color

3. Have students select a television quiz show format and use the information in a classroom display of graphic aids as the basis for their questions.

4. Have students use their graphic aids to put together a bound book that can be housed in the school library.

5. Have students complete a teacher-prepared scavenger hunt using information found in a classroom display of graphic aids.

TEACHING HINTS:
1. You may choose to give students a group assignment for constructing a graphic aid. Many of the following activities work well as cooperative learning experiences.

2. Through our experience with students, we have learned that, although innate artistic ability is an asset, it is not a prerequisite to producing work of high quality. However, it is imperative that a student be given guidance, encouragement, and creative license in keeping with his or her communicative purpose. A student who feels limited in artistic ability should emphasize illustrations that can be drawn easily with the use of a ruler, compass, or a few simple lines. In addition, this student could be encouraged to incorporate cut-out pictures and to concentrate on lettering and the presentation of written information in the graphic aid.

AN ADVERTISING CAMPAIGN

OBJECTIVE: Creating an original character to be used in a mock advertising campaign to educate the public

MATERIALS: For this activity, you will need posterboard, resource materials, and markers or colored pencils.

PROCEDURE:

1. Choose a topic that interests you, then find out more about the topic. Keep notes of interesting and unusual information as well as basic facts to inform your audience. Determine what elements are associated with the topic. For example, if the topic was nutrition, the following elements would be related: breads, cereals, meat, fish, poultry, milk, cheese, fruits, vegetables, and fat.

2. Create a character to be a spokesperson for your topic. Make the character's appearance and name indicative of the topic.

3. Use your character in a poster that will tell your classmates about your topic. You may want to look through magazine ads for advertising techniques that may give you ideas.

IT'S POLITICAL

OBJECTIVE: Creating an original political cartoon to convey an opinion on a current issue

MATERIALS: For this activity, you will need posterboard and markers or colored pencils.

PROCEDURE:

1. Choose an issue in your life about which you have a strong opinion, such as homework, tests, cafeteria food, nuclear energy, toxic waste, politics, etc. Think of something that annoys you, something you believe is unfair, or something you believe should be changed.

2. Design a political cartoon that portrays your personal gripe. Remember that a political cartoon uses exaggeration to get its message across. Consider the following elements when creating your political cartoon:

   • people   • title
   • objects   • words, phrases, and sentences
   • symbols   • dates and numbers
   • captions

3. Use the space below to make a rough sketch of your cartoon before finalizing your work on the posterboard.

A LITERARY SCENE

OBJECTIVE: Illustrating a scene from literature

MATERIALS: For this activity, you will need posterboard, scrap paper, and markers or colored pencils.

PROCEDURE:

1. From your reading choose a scene to illustrate. Try to visualize this scene.

2. Give thought to the important details that would help bring this scene to life in a poster: clues as to time and place of the scene, characters and their expressions.

3. You will want to include in this poster the title of the literary selection, its author, and a caption that explains the importance of this scene to the rest of the story.

4. Below is an example of such a scene from *Tom Sawyer*.

5. Now, on a sheet of scrap paper, complete a rough draft of your poster. Be sure to include all the necessary elements.

6. Once you have your rough draft done and your ideas worked out, begin your final copy on the posterboard.

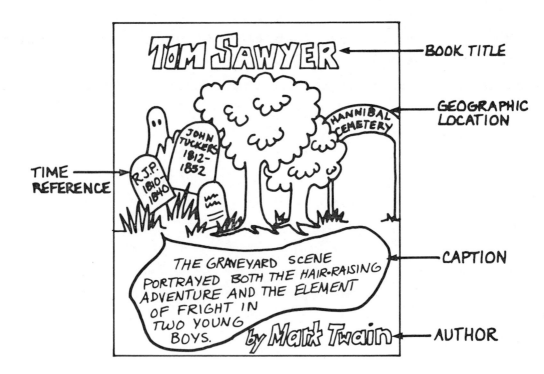

INDEX CARD ILLUSTRATIONS

OBJECTIVE: Completing an index card presentation of a record or an interesting or unusual fact.

MATERIALS: For this activity, you will need a pencil, $3'' \times 5''$ unlined index cards, and fine-tip markers.

PROCEDURE:

1. Find an interesting fact or record you would like to share with the class.

2. Decide on a title for your card. Center your title on the left half of the card. Print it in all capital letters. Underline the title and go over the lettering with a fine-tip marker.

3. Using a fine-tip marker, print the explanation or description of the record or fact. This goes under the title. You may want to lightly sketch in lines to allow your lettering to be straight. You then erase these lines before finishing. This printing is to be done in fine-line marker. (Be sure sentence structure and mechanics have all been edited before writing on the card.)

4. Using a variety of color markers, draw your illustration in the space on the right side of the card. The illustration should be done as well as possible. If you are not an artist, draw a very simple picture. Your illustration should take up most of the space.

EXTENSION: Use your card as part of a class display.

MONOPOLY®, Game Equipment used with permission from Parker Brothers
© 1935, 1985

DIAGRAMING A PROCESS

OBJECTIVE: Drawing a diagram to illustrate a process

MATERIALS: For this activity, you will need scrap paper, posterboard, and markers or colored pencils.

PROCEDURE:

1. Decide on a process or operation that can be portrayed through a diagram.
2. Identify the sequence of steps involved in completing the process.
3. Plan a rough sketch of this process that includes words, symbols, and illustrations.
4. Prepare a final copy of your diagram. Use of color will not only enhance the visual presentation, but can also aid in clarifying the procedure.

WHEN WAS IT?

OBJECTIVE: Constructing a timeline consisting of information and illustrations concerning a chosen topic

MATERIALS: For this activity, you will need colored pencils or markers and posterboard.

PROCEDURE:

1. Select a topic to research.

2. Identify significant events associated with this topic. Record dates, events, and relevant information.

3. Determine the earliest and latest dates and calibrate a timeline accordingly. This calibration may be in hours, days, weeks, months, years, decades, centuries, etc. Each time calibration must be spaced evenly from the ones before and after it.

4. Illustrate your timeline. Below is a sample timeline that relates to automobile history.

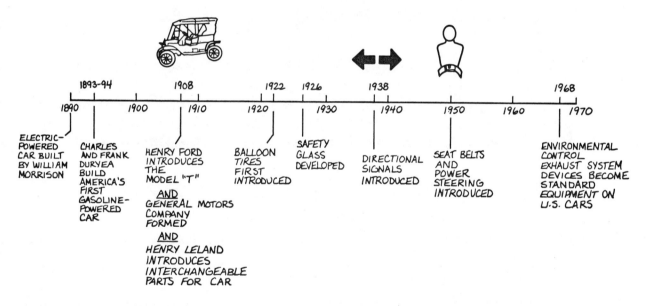

SIGNIFICANT DATES IN
AMERICAN
AUTOMOBILE HISTORY

SKILL: B. Tables and Graphs

OBJECTIVE:
Students will complete a variety of activities to help develop their communication skills through the use of tables and graphs.

STRATEGIES:
1. Review with students the forms of various tables and graphs through the use of overhead transparencies. For different types of tables and graphs, lead students to identify each part and its function.

2. When students are constructing a table, discuss with them the data to be shown. Have them identify the examples that will be listed vertically in the first column. Then help students identify the characteristics that will label each succeeding column. Finally, have students complete the table.

3. When students are constructing a line or bar graph, discuss with them the data to be shown. Help students conclude that the Y axis usually shows a scale of measurement (linear, time, weight, temperature, volume, etc.). The X axis usually shows examples that have been measured. Point out that all graphs have a title; some may include a legend explaining features on the graph.

4. Before students construct circle graphs, you may need to review or teach some necessary math skills. Students are required to compute percentages and to use a protractor and a compass. If you give students the percentages, they will not need to compute them.

5. Have students design a rough draft of the graph or table. This will allow the student to visualize and to organize the thoughts to be communicated. Discuss with students their use of different types, sizes, and colors of lettering. Large, bold lettering may be used to indicate greater importance whereas smaller lettering may indicate details.

6. It will be helpful to your students if you provide a set of directions or checklists specific to the assignment. Your directions/checklist may direct students to include the following:
   - title
   - labeled parts
   - appropriate lettering
   - color

7. Direct students to use rulers, compasses, and protractors when necessary.

8. Have students prepare a scavenger hunt, crossword puzzle, question sheet, etc. that can then be traded and answered by another student.

TEACHING HINTS:

1. You may choose to give students a group assignment for constructing a graphic aid. Many of the following activities work well as cooperative learning experiences.

2. You may choose to have students present the same data in two different forms, such as a table and a written narrative. Then students can discuss the advantages and disadvantages of each form.

ANSWERS:

IVB-2 Drawing a Bar Graph

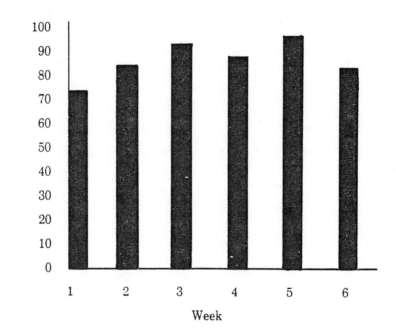

IVB-3 Drawing a Line Graph

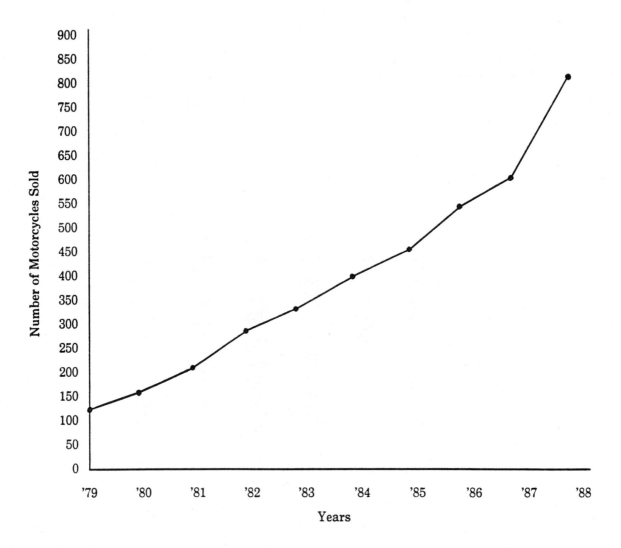

IVB-4 Drawing a Circle Graph
2. a. soda
   b. popcorn
   c. lunch
   d. movies
   e. model plane
3. a. 5%
   b. 7.5%
   c. 22.5%

        d. 30%

        e. 35%

4. a. 18 degrees

     b. 27 degrees

     c. 81 degrees

     d. 108 degrees

     e. 126 degrees

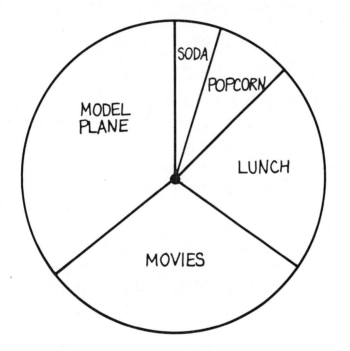

IV. CONSTRUCTING GRAPHIC AIDS   B. Tables and Graphs

PRESENTING INFORMATION THROUGH A TABLE

OBJECTIVE: Constructing a table to present information about a particular topic

MATERIALS: For this activity, you will need posterboard, a ruler, and markers or colored pencils.

PROCEDURE:

1.   Choose a topic for which you can think of at least six examples, such as planets, the New England States, or football teams.

2.   Construct a table labeling the first column with the topic. Write the examples in the first column. Label the additional columns with categories of information you will find and present. Possible categories for a table about planets could include the following: size, distance from the sun, atmosphere, number of moons, length of day, or length of year.

3.   Draw the vertical lines to create the columns for your table.

4.   Locate the necessary information to complete the table.

© 1990 by The Center for Applied Research in Education

IV. CONSTRUCTING GRAPHIC AIDS   B. Tables and Graphs

DRAWING A BAR GRAPH

OBJECTIVE: Organizing information and constructing a bar graph

MATERIALS: For this activity, you will need a pencil, colored pencils, and a ruler.

PROCEDURE:

1. In this activity, you will present the data given in the form of a bar graph. Study the information below:

> Maria has taken a weekly spelling test for the past six weeks. You will show her progress by graphing her results in a bar graph. Here are her scores for a six-week period.
>
> Week 1 — 72%
> Week 2 — 83%
> Week 3 — 92%
> Week 4 — 87%
> Week 5 — 94%
> Week 6 — 82%

2. Above week 1 on the graph below, draw a bar that extends up to a little beyond the 70% mark. Shade in the bar. Do the same for the remaining five weeks.

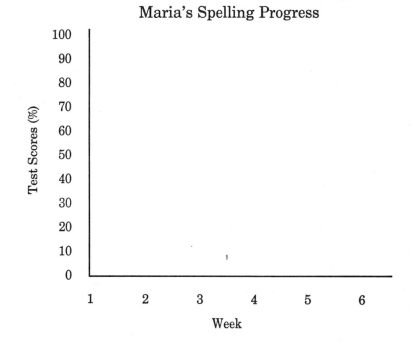

Maria's Spelling Progress

EXTENSION: Construct a bar graph for another set of data. Bar graphs allow the reader to easily see comparisons/contrasts.

DRAWING A LINE GRAPH

OBJECTIVE: Organizing information and constructing a line graph

MATERIALS: For this activity, you will need a pencil and a ruler.

PROCEDURE: In this activity, you will present given data in the form of a line graph. Study the information below, then complete the line graph.

The Deals in Wheels Shop is interested in studying its motorcycle sales for the last ten years. Here is a listing of the number of motorcycles sold for a ten-year period.

1979 — 125	1984 — 390
1980 — 155	1985 — 450
1981 — 210	1986 — 550
1982 — 285	1987 — 600
1983 — 325	1988 — 800

Motorcycle Sales for 1979–1988
at the Deals in Wheels Shop

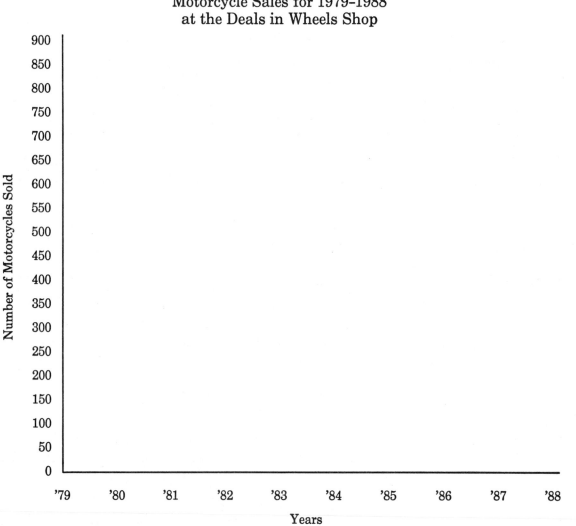

IVB-3

DRAWING A LINE GRAPH (continued)

EXTENSION: Construct a line graph for another set of data. Line graphs are good for showing change over time.

DRAWING A CIRCLE GRAPH

OBJECTIVE: Organizing information and constructing a circle graph

MATERIALS: For this activity, you will need a pencil, a protractor, and a ruler.

PROCEDURE:

1. In this activity, you will present given data in the form of a circle graph. Study the information below.

> Rick received ten dollars for his birthday. He spent his money in the following way:
>
> Movies $3.00
> Popcorn .... .75
> Soda .... .50
> Lunch 2.25
> Model plane 3.50

2. Arrange these items below from lowest priced to highest priced.

a. _____ (lowest priced)

b. _____

c. _____

d. _____

e. _____ (highest priced)

3. The circle graph is a fine way to show how Rick spent his ten dollars. First, you must find the percent of the total ten dollars that each item represents. In order to do this, divide the price of each item by the total amount of ten dollars. Compute this information and put your results here.

a. Movies .... $3.00/$10.00 = _____

b. Popcorn .... 0.75/$10.00 = _____

c. Soda .... 0.50/$10.00 = _____

d. Lunch .... 2.25/$10.00 = _____

e. Model plane .... 3.50/$10.00 = _____

4. Once you have determined the percentage for each item, multiply it by 360 degrees to find the number of degrees within the circle needed to represent the item. Place the number of degrees needed for each item here.

© 1990 by The Center for Applied Research in Education

DRAWING A CIRCLE GRAPH (continued)

    a. Movies   _____ degrees

    b. Popcorn   _____ degrees

    c. Soda   _____ degrees

    d. Lunch   _____ degrees

    e. Model plane   _____ degrees

5. Take the first item: soda. Beginning at the 360-degree mark, count up to the number of necessary degrees for this item. Draw two lines: one from the center of the circle to the 360-degree mark and one from the center of the circle to the mark for the proper number of degrees. Label the inside of this wedge SODA.

6. Follow this same procedure with the remaining four items. Go in order from lowest percentage to highest percentage. Move the protractor to start at 360° for each item.

Rick's Spending of His Birthday Money

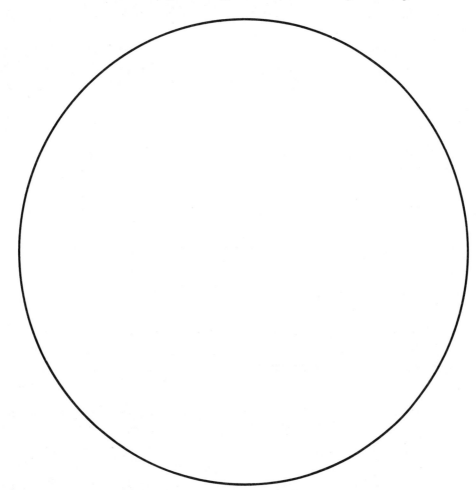

SKILL: C. Maps and Models

OBJECTIVE:
Students will complete a variety of activities to help develop their communication skills through the use of maps and models.

STRATEGIES:
1. Review with students the purpose of maps. Maps are a representation of a location. They may show a variety of information including weather conditions, transportation routes, water bodies, land forms, and political regions.

2. Review with students the elements of a map: symbols, legends, scale, and title.

3. Prior to students drawing maps, you may want to involve them in computing distance using a scale.

4. Direct students to design a rough draft of their maps, allowing them to organize the elements.

5. It will be helpful to your students if you provide a set of directions/ checklist specific to the assignment. The checklist may direct students to include the following:
    *   title
    *   scale
    *   symbols
    *   legend
    *   color
    *   labels

6. Review with students the purpose of models as a three-dimensional representation of an object, event, place, location, or idea. Models vary in their forms and functions. For example, some may include labels, some may have moving parts, and some may show interaction.

SPECIAL DIRECTIONS:
"Creating Models": Give the class a scale to use, such as 1 inch = 1 foot. Have each student create a fold-up home or commercial building. Use these structures to create a town or commercial setting.

TEACHING HINTS:
1. You may choose to give students a group assignment for constructing a graphic aid. Many of the following activities work well as cooperative learning experiences.

2. You may choose to have students use their prepared graphic aids in a presentation or display to one, a few, or many other people. This can be especially effective if students prepare a presentation for a group of younger students, students in other classes, or for groups outside of school (senior citizens, parent groups, community groups).

Name _____ Date _____

IV. CONSTRUCTING GRAPHIC AIDS   *C. Maps and Models*

HOW DO I GET TO SCHOOL?

OBJECTIVE: Constructing a map that shows the shortest route between a student's home and school

MATERIALS: For this activity, you will need unlined paper, markers or colored pencils, and a ruler.

PROCEDURE:

1. In the space below, use symbols to indicate your home, your school, and landmarks between them. Fill in the names of the streets on which you travel to get to school. Include turns you make and curves in the roads. Make a legend to show each symbol and its meaning.

2. Make a final copy of your map on unlined paper, adjusting the distances if necessary.

IV. CONSTRUCTING GRAPHIC AIDS   C. Maps and Models

A THREE-DIMENSIONAL MAP

OBJECTIVE: Constructing a three-dimensional map

MATERIALS: For this activity, you will need paper, scissors, markers, a sturdy piece of cardboard or piece of wood, plaster of Paris or modeling clay or a mixture of flour/salt/water to build up the elevations, and other objects to represent landscape features, water areas, automobiles, etc.

PROCEDURE:

1. Choose a location for which you will construct a three-dimensional map.

2. Determine if there are any landforms that must be included, such as continents, rivers, lakes, mountains, hills, craters, etc. Sketch the location of the landforms on the cardboard or wood base.

3. Form the elevations on the cardboard or wood base. After the elevations have dried, construct or gather materials to represent any other three-dimensional aspects of your map. Evergreen twigs, for example, may be used for trees or forests. Paper or cardboard can be used to make buildings, and small toys can be included for cars, people, and/or animals.

4. Make labels to clarify the parts of your map.

IV. CONSTRUCTING GRAPHIC AIDS   C. Maps and Models

CONSTRUCTING A SCALE DRAWING

OBJECTIVE: Constructing a scale map of a furnished room

MATERIALS: For this activity, you will need a pencil, a measuring stick or tape, a ruler, graph paper, and scrap paper.

PROCEDURE:

1. Using a measuring stick or tape, compute the length and width of the room you have chosen to draw.

   Room's length = _____

   Room's width = _____

2. Measure the width of doorway openings and window sills. (Remember, this map will be of a top view. Therefore, we will want to show windows and doorway openings around the room's perimeter.)

   Width of windows: _____

   Width of doorways: _____

3. List all pieces of furniture within the room and list their dimensions (length and width) as you would see the furniture from a top view.

Furniture	Length	Width

4. Make a rough drawing of the room on scrap paper. Include all doorways, windows, and furniture. On the map of the room, put in the various dimensions.

5. Now you are ready to complete your scale drawing on the graph paper. Remember, neatness and accuracy are important in this final copy.

6. Decide upon your scale. For example, a quarter of an inch equals one foot on the sample map shown.

CONSTRUCTING A SCALE DRAWING (continued)

7. Center your room on the graph paper. Draw in the perimeter of the room (length and width).
8. Draw in the doorways and windows.
9. Draw in the various pieces of furniture.
10. Label all the measurements.
11. Label all the items in the room in capital letters.
12. Put the scale on the map in a lower corner that shows what distance on the map equals what distance on the scale drawing.
13. Put the title on the map at the top and be sure it is in all capital letters and centered.

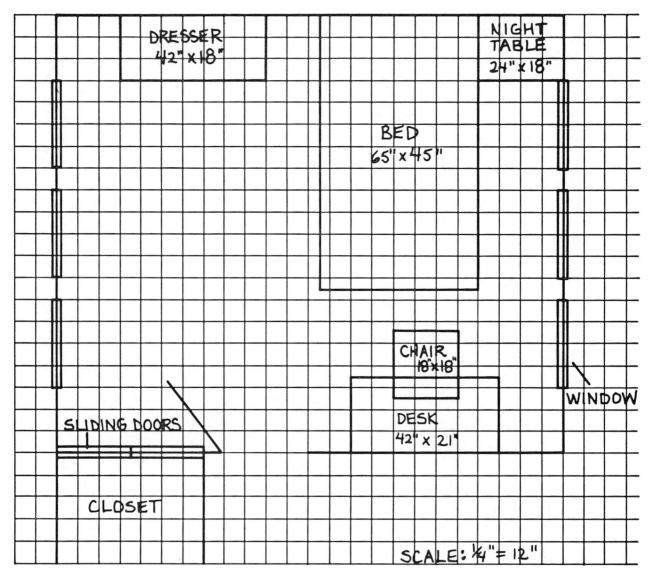

DRESSER 42" x 18"

NIGHT TABLE 24" x 18"

BED 65" x 45"

NIGHT TABLE 24" x 18"

CHAIR 18"x18"

WINDOW

SLIDING DOORS

DESK 42" x 21"

CLOSET

SCALE: ¼" = 12"

CONSTRUCTING A MODEL TO INFORM AN AUDIENCE

OBJECTIVE: Using a model to explain a vocabulary term or content area concept

MATERIALS: For this activity, you will need art materials to construct a model.

PROCEDURE:

1.   Choose a vocabulary term or concept that you will explain through a model such as a volcano, cooperation, division, or analogies.

2.   Construct a model that shows the meaning of the vocabulary term or concept.

3.   Label the parts or stages included in your model.

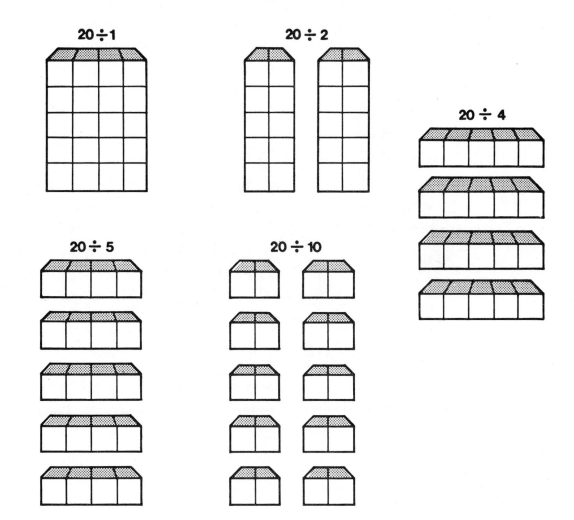

IV. CONSTRUCTING GRAPHIC AIDS   *C. Maps and Models*

CREATING A MODEL OF AN EVENT

OBJECTIVE: Illustrating an event through a model

MATERIALS: For this activity, you will need art materials for creating the model and a cardboard or wooden base upon which to build the model.

PROCEDURE:

1. Choose an event from history, from your life, or from fiction which you will portray in a model.

2. Construct a model or diagram showing the event. Be sure to include standing figures or objects on a base which show the location of the event.

3. Label your model. If necessary, label the stages to show the sequence of the event. Include labels and information to help your classmates understand the significance of the model and its parts.

IV. CONSTRUCTING GRAPHIC AIDS   C. Maps and Models

CREATING MODELS

OBJECTIVE: Constructing a fold-up housing structure

MATERIALS: For this activity, you will need the pattern, a pencil, scissors, and glue or tape.

PROCEDURE:

1. Cut out the pattern along the solid lines.
2. Fold along the dotted lines so that the flaps are positioned within the structure.
3. Carefully glue or tape the flaps into position. You will need to use the floor opening in this process.
4. As a class, these models may be used as the basis for a scale community.

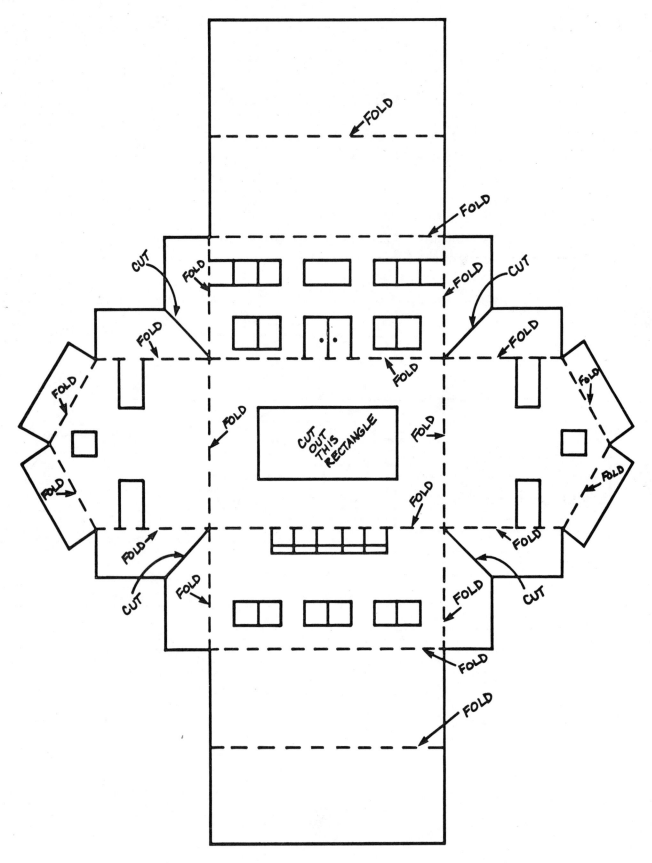

CUT OUT THIS RECTANGLE

IVC-6 (continued)